Developing Number Sense Grades 3–6

Rusty Bresser
Caren Holtzman

MATH SOLUTIONS PUBLICATIONS
Sausalito, California

Math Solutions Publications
A division of
Marilyn Burns Education Associates
150 Gate 5 Road, Suite 101
Sausalito, CA 94965
www.mathsolutions.com

Library of Congress Cataloging-in-Publication Data
Bresser, Rusty.
    Developing number sense : grades 3–6 / Rusty Bresser and Caren
Holtzman.
        p.   cm.
    ISBN 0-941355-23-3 (pbk.)
    1. Number concept.   2. Mathematics—Study and teaching
(Elementary)   I. Holtzman, Caren.   II. Title.
    QA141.15.B74   1999
    372.7'2044—dc21   99-23644
                                                            CIP

Oh No! 99! is adapted from a UNO Company game, now out of print.

Tell Me All You Can is adapted from *Smart Arithmetic, Grades 4–6,* by Rhea Irvine and Kathryn Walker (Creative Publications).

Stand Up and Be Counted was created by Annette Raphel, Shady Hill School, Cambridge, Massachusetts.

Get to 1,000, Get to Zero, and Hit the Target are adapted from *Calculators in Mathematics Education* (NCTM Yearbook) (Reston, VA: National Council of Teachers of Mathematics, 1992).

Editor: Toby Gordon
Copy editor: Alan Huisman

Production: Alan Huisman
Book design and illustrations: Joni Doherty
Cover design: Leslie Bauman

Composition: Cape Cod Compositors, Inc.

Printed in the United States of America
09 08 07 06 05   ML   5 6 7 8 9

A Message from Marilyn Burns

We at Marilyn Burns Education Associates believe that teaching mathematics well calls for increasing our understanding of the math we teach, seeking greater insight into how children learn mathematics, and refining lessons to best promote children's learning. All of our Math Solutions Professional Development publications and inservice courses have been designed to help teachers achieve these goals.

Our publications include a wide range of choices, from books in our new Teaching Arithmetic and Lessons for Algebraic Thinking series to resources that link math and literacy; from books to help teachers understand mathematics more deeply to children's books that help students develop an appreciation for math while learning basic concepts.

Our inservice programs offer five-day courses, one-day workshops, and series of school-year sessions throughout the country, working in partnership with school districts to help implement and sustain long-term improvement in mathematics instruction in all classrooms.

To find a complete listing of our publications and workshops, please visit our Web site at *www.mathsolutions.com*. Or contact us by calling (800) 868-9092 or sending an e-mail to *info@mathsolutions.com*.

We're eager for your feedback and interested in learning about your particular needs. We look forward to hearing from you.

Math
SOLUTIONS®
Publications
A DIVISION OF MARILYN BURNS EDUCATION ASSOCIATES

Contents

Acknowledgments

We thank the following people for making this book possible:

Marilyn Burns, for her guidance and support
Toby Gordon and Alan Huisman, for their editorial expertise
Andrea Barraugh
Sherry Beard
Dina Calvin
Shea Carrillo
Julie Contestable
Ann Dominick
Carolyn Felux
Marji Freeman
Kathleen Gallagher
Sally Haggerty
Pam Long
Lyndsey Lovelace
Annette Raphel
Patti Reynolds
Christina Stamford
Serena Thakur
Maryann Wickett
Pam Wilson

And special thanks to Alberto Bautista

Introduction

Two children eating dinner at a kitchen table argue about whose plate has more peas on it. A man in a checkout line thumbs through the money in his wallet, deciding whether he has enough cash to pay for his groceries. A woman filling the gas tank of her car wonders how many miles she drives per gallon. A student taking a test estimates a reasonable solution to $8/9 + 7/8$. A teenager glances at the clock: does he have time to stop by his friend's house before heading home for dinner?

Solving these sorts of everyday problems requires number sense. Number sense is extremely important to our mathematical thinking and reasoning. Starting from a very young age, we're confronted with situation after situation in which we need to think about and use numbers.

Number sense is a broad idea that covers a range of numerical thinking. Although the concept can be difficult to pinpoint, we recognize number sense when we see our students use it.

Our students with number sense understand the relationships between and among numbers. They think flexibly about numbers, are able to break numbers apart and put them together in a variety of ways. They are also familiar with the properties of single-digit numbers and can use this information to calculate efficiently using larger numbers.

Students with number sense also understand the effects operations have on numbers. They see connections between the different operations and have a firm grasp on which operation or series of operations to employ in a given situation. They are able to articulate why they choose a particular operation and how it will help them solve the problem.

Another component of number sense is mental computation. Students with number sense can manipulate numbers in their head. They have strategies they use to think about numbers and operations. They do not need to rely solely on paper and pencil, their fingers, or a calculator. Also, students with number sense have effective ways to estimate. They can approximate calculations and use familiar benchmarks to gauge unknown amounts.

While there is no simple checklist of skills that number sense encompasses, we recognize its components and its effects. We see our students use their number sense when they are confronted with numerical situations. We hear them describe their number sense when they explain how they solved a problem. As Paul R. Trafton puts it, "A person who possesses number sense might be said to have a well-integrated mental map of a portion of the world of numbers and operations and is able to move flexibly and intuitively throughout the territory" ("Using Number Sense to Develop Mental Computation and Computational Estimation," paper presented at a conference entitled Challenging Children to Think When They Compute, Queensland University of Technology, Brisbane Australia, August 9–11, 1991).

This book shows some of the ways we have attempted to help students "move throughout the territory." It offers practical and worthwhile ideas for helping students think about numbers. It will help you understand number sense and find innovative ways to promote it in your classroom.

Over a two-year span, we taught each of these activities in an intermediate classroom. In most instances, we taught the activity more than once, to different grade levels, in order to refine and polish it and

determine how to modify or adapt it to meet the needs of different-aged students. We have integrated assessment ideas into the activities because we recognize that teachers assess their students continually. In these pages we share what we learned from the students during the activities and how we feel the activities helped the children enhance their number sense.

The activities in the book are grouped into four sections: Mental Computation, The Basics and More, Navigating the Number System, and Estimation. A brief introduction to each section highlights the key number-sense ideas that group of activities is intended to develop.

The activities are of several different types. Some are games that the teacher introduces to the whole class and then has the students play in pairs or in small groups. Some are investigations that are introduced to the whole class, after which students carry them out individually, in pairs, or in small groups. Some activities don't lead to individual or small-group work but are whole-class experiences only.

Each activity has three components:

1. A concise summary.
2. An extended vignette that describes how we taught the activity in a classroom.
3. Answers to one or more reflective questions.

There is no prescribed way to use the book or the activities: this is not a program, curriculum, or sequential unit. Rather, it is a spectrum of ways to foster number sense in the intermediate grades. If you are just beginning to focus on number sense in your classroom, we hope you will find here practical ideas and insights into the richness and power of number sense. If you are already focusing on number sense, we hope you will find some activities and perspectives to add to your repertoire. We encourage you to use the activities in ways that best meet the needs of your students, and we'd appreciate hearing about your experiences and any adaptations you try as you go about bringing number sense to the forefront of your mathematics instruction.

Mental Computation

While many of the activities in this book rely on mental computation, these first three focus heavily on it. In Get to 1,000, Oh No! 99!, and Get to Zero students engage in games and investigations that require mental computation. The discussions and written work students engage in after the activities also focus on their mental computation strategies. While the discussions and conversations in the vignettes that follow won't be replicated exactly in your classroom, they are models for how teachers can focus on and foster students' mental strategies.

Mental computation is a key aspect of number sense. It forces students to rely on what they know about numbers and operations. It also liberates them from the standard paper-and-pencil approach to computation and allows them to be more inventive. Computing mentally shifts the emphasis from following procedures to making sense of numbers and operations. It allows students to develop their own algorithms.

For example, if a group of students had to compute 39 + 44 mentally, one student might take 1 from 44 and use it to turn the 39 into 40, then add 40 and 43. Another student might start with the tens and add 30 and 40, which makes 70, then add the 9 and the 4 to get 13, then add 70 and 13 to get 83. The activities in this section give students many opportunities to come up with their own computing methods, thus helping them develop their number sense.

As always, the teacher's role is vital. Our goal is to help students become flexible thinkers who are comfortable with numbers and who are able to compute accurately and efficiently. But asking students merely to give an answer they've computed in their head limits their potential to develop number sense. The thinking leading to the answer is also important. Teachers need to encourage students to discuss their methods in class; that way the students expose one another to a wide array of strategies, gradually becoming more flexible and facile with numbers and operations. The activities here encourage these kinds of classroom conversations.

1 *Get to 1,000*

Overview

This two-person game gives students practice with multiplying by powers of ten and with addition. Players multiply the number that comes up on each of ten rolls of the die by 1, 10, or 100. Then they add the ten products. The total may be under or over 1,000. The player whose final score is closer to 1,000 is the winner. Variations of the game give students practice multiplying by 5, 25, and 50.

Materials Needed

One die for each pair of students.

Directions for Playing the Game

1. Players, in pairs, take turns rolling a die. On each roll, each player decides separately whether he or she wants to multiply the number on the die by 1, 10, or 100.
2. Each player records the resulting product on a piece of paper.
3. Players continue to roll, multiply, and record their products until they each have ten products on their paper. (Each player will have rolled the die five times.)
4. Each player finds the sum of his or her products. The one whose final score is closer to 1,000, whether over or under, is the winner.

Extensions

1. Version A: roll the die ten times and multiply the number on the die by 1, 5, or 50.
2. Version B: roll the die ten times and multiply the number on the die by 10, 25, or 50.
3. Version C: roll the die seven times and multiply the number on the die by 1, 10, or 100.

IN THE CLASSROOM WITH RUSTY

Introducing the Activity

I told Kathleen Gallagher's fourth graders I wanted to teach them a game called Get to 1,000 that involved multiplication, addition, and subtraction. After I showed them how, they'd be able to play it with a partner.

"For this game, you want to get as close to 1,000 as possible," I began. "You may go over or under 1,000, but you want to get as close as you can. Each time you roll the die, you have a choice whether to multiply the number on the die by one, ten, or 100." I wrote × *1,* × *10,* × *100* on the chalkboard. "Each time I get another product, I'll write it down on a piece of paper. As I play the game, I'll try to keep track of my score in my head so that I'll know about how close I am to 1,000. After ten rolls, I'll add up the products and see how close to 1,000 I get." I noticed some blank looks. "I'll roll the die, and you can watch me to see how the game is played," I told them. "I'll ask for suggestions from you along the way."

I rolled the die and got a four. "I can multiply four by one, ten, or 100," I said, thinking out loud. "I'm going to choose to multiply four by 100. What's four times 100?"

"Four hundred!" the class chorused.

"How do you know that?" I asked.

"Because you take four and add two zeros," said Elias. "Four times 100 means you do four 100 times."

"It's like 400 pennies," added Brad.

"Look, you skip count by 100s," Nadine pointed out matter-of-factly.

"Let's try that together and see if it works," I suggested. Together we counted by 100s to 400. As we counted, I realized that for a great many children in the class, the answer to 4×100 was obvious. I also knew that this part of our discussion could give some of them different ways to think about multiplication. The mathematical understanding of the students in the room varied from solid to extremely fragile.

I wrote *400* on the chalkboard and rolled again. This time I got a six. "I'm going to multiply six times ten this time," I said. "Can someone explain why that might be a good choice?" Lots of hands popped up, and I called on Cathy.

"Well, if you multiplied six times 100 you'd get 600, and that would put you at 1,000 already," she explained. "So six times ten is a good move. I think you could multiply six times one and that would also be a good move."

"What's six times ten?" I asked the class.

"Sixty!" they said together.

"Can someone explain how you know that six times ten is 60?" I asked. I wanted the students to know that I was interested in more than correct answers. I wanted them to explain their ideas in order to increase the learning potential.

"Because ten six times is 60," said Sharon.

"You can count by ten six times," explained Jim.

"It's like six dimes," offered Simon.

I wrote *60* on the chalkboard underneath the *400*. I rolled again and got a one. I multiplied 1 × 100 and wrote *100* under the *60*. I then rolled another six.

"What should I do now?" I asked. "Any advice?"

"I think you should multiply by ten because you already have over 500, and if you multiply by 100 you'll go over 1,000, because 600 and 500 is 1,100," Sue explained.

"Does that make sense?" I asked. Students nodded their head in agreement, and I added another *60* to the list of figures on the board.

I rolled again and got a two. I multiplied 2 × 10 and wrote *20* on the chalkboard under the other products. I now had *400, 60, 100, 60,* and *20* on the chalkboard. We had just finished our fifth roll and we were halfway to the finish.

"I'd like you to figure the score in your head," I instructed. "When we calculate mentally it helps improve our math thinking. Also, if we keep track of our scores as we go along, we'll know how close to 1,000 we are." After a moment, I called on Marcos.

"It's 640, because 400 plus 100 equals 500, then I added 60 plus 60 equals 120, then I added 20 more, equals 140; 500 plus 140 equals 640," he explained.

"Did anyone figure it a different way?" I probed.

"I did it almost the same way," Rob began. "After I added 400 and 100 to get 500, I looked at the two 60s and saw two 50s. That made another 100. Then I had 600 and just added

the 20 and the two 10s I took from the two 60s."

I was pleased that Rob was able to "see" that 60 could be broken down into 50 + 10 and how he used that to make the problem easier for him to solve. The ability to take numbers apart and put them back together is an indicator of number sense.

On my next roll, I got a two and multiplied it by ten and recorded *20* on the chalkboard. Then I rolled a one and again asked the class for advice.

"I think you should multiply it by 100," said Brad.

"Why do you think that?" I asked.

"Because you only have four rolls left and you only have 660," he reasoned. "If you had rolled a higher number, I'd advise you to multiply by ten or one."

I continued with the game until I had ten products written on the chalkboard. "Raise your hand if you have an idea about how to find the total," I said. I waited till lots of hands were raised, then called on Calvin.

"Add the 100s, then the tens, then the ones," he suggested. "It's easier to start clumping together the bigger numbers. Anyway, the numbers are pretty friendly."

"Use a calculator," added Kimm.

"You can make 100s," observed Adela. "Like 60 and 40 is 100, so I'd make as many 100s as I could, then go to the lower numbers. I'd add everything together in my mind."

After we found the sum of the products, students partnered up to play Get to 1,000. Before they began, I reminded them that both players had to use the same number on the die when multiplying and that they each had to make separate decisions about what to do. I told them that partners had to roll the die ten times and that at the end of the game, the player whose score was closer to 1,000 won. I also told them that keeping track of their score as they played the game was important. They could do this mentally or on a piece of paper.

Observing the Students

As students played I walked from table to table, listening to conversations, posing questions, and making observations. Rob and Charles were on their final roll when I joined their game.

"I've got 800. I'm getting close," Charles said.

He was thinking out loud and was ready to make the final roll when I stopped him with my question: "What would have to happen for you to make 1,000 exactly?"

Charles thought for a while. Rob was dying to answer, but I put up my hand, signaling him to be patient and give Charles a chance.

"Hmm. I need 200 more to make 1,000. If I rolled a one and multiplied by 100, I'd get 900, so if I rolled a two and multiplied it by 100, I'd get there exactly," he reasoned.

"Do you think it's likely that someone would get 1,000 exactly?" I asked.

Charles and Rob looked at each other, not quite sure how to respond. Leaving them to think about this question, I moved on to another table.

Ramon and Adela were having a disagreement about who won the game.

"I got 1,006, and you got 964, so I won!" argued Ramon.

"How do you know that?" Adela shot back. "It looks to me like we're both close to 1,000."

"You're farther away than me!" he countered. I held back and watched, not interfering. "Look, 1,006 is only six away from 1,000," Ramon said firmly. "Nine hundred and sixty-four is . . . ," he began.

"Wait, I want to figure it out!" Adela insisted. "Nine hundred and seventy-four, 984, 994, that's 30 and six more . . . oops, you're closer!" They both giggled.

Their responses had given me some insight into their number sense. Ramon exuded confidence about using numbers to solve problems. Although Adela seemed less sure of herself, she did have the confidence to insist on figuring things out for herself.

A Class Discussion

When it seemed as though most partners had completed two games, I asked for everyone's attention and initiated a class discussion.

"When you're playing Get to 1,000, what do you think about in order to win the game?" I asked.

"Well, first I multiplied by 100, then I multiplied the numbers on the die by ten, then by one," said Jenny.

"Why did you do that?" I asked.

"I learned that you should try to get to 900 as fast as you can and then go to small tens and big ones," Jenny explained. "The way to get to 900 is to multiply first by 100."

"Other strategies?" I asked.

"My strategy was doing about five 100s as long as the numbers are low, occasionally some ones, and the rest tens," Brandy reported. "If I rolled sixes a lot and multiplied by 100, I'd be in trouble 'cause that would put me way over 1,000."

"If you multiplied every number that came up on the die by 100, do you think you'd win?" I asked.

"Not if I rolled sixes every time," Jenny responded. "That would get you . . ." She stopped to think.

"What are you thinking?" I asked.

"I'm trying to add 600 ten times, because the biggest number you can get on one roll is 600 and if you did that ten times . . . I'm stuck," she said.

"What can you say about the answer to 600 times ten?" I asked the class. I gave them a little time to think about this, then called on Simone.

"I think it's going to be bigger than 1,000 because 600 times two is 1,200," said Simone. Simone was using something she knew, 600×2, to think about the magnitude of the answer to 600×10. She was tapping into her number sense to think about the problem.

"Anyone else have an idea?" I asked.

"I'm skip counting by sixes and if you go 6, 12, 18, 24 . . . that would be 600 times four is 2,400, so it's bigger than that," Brandy reasoned. "So 600 times eight is double that." Brandy's thinking often kept the class on their toes. She was very capable and comfortable with numbers.

I wanted as many students as possible to see Brandy's line of reasoning, so I asked a probing question. "Brandy said that 600 times four is 2,400 so 600 times eight is double that," I clarified. "Think about what 600 times eight might be, then tell someone next to you."

After a moment, I asked for their attention and called on Jenny.

"Well, 600 times eight is 4,800 'cause if 600 times four is 2,400 then 2,400 plus 2,400 is 4,800," she explained.

"So what about 600 times ten?" I asked.

"It's a little more than 4,800, maybe a couple hundred more," said Rob.

"It's 6,000!" Kimm exclaimed. "I kept adding 600 in my head ten times."

"You can get 1,000 exactly if you keep rolling ones and multiplying by 100!" Ramon exclaimed, jumping into the conversation.

"Is that likely to happen?" I asked. Most students shook their head no.

"I wonder if there's another way to get 1,000?" Brandy thought out loud.

"That's an interesting question we could investigate later," I said. I knew we wouldn't have time to pursue the question today, but it indicated the rich potential of the game.

A Writing Assignment

At the end of our discussion, I asked the students to write about what they learned while playing Get to 1,000. I also asked them to write about their strategies for winning.

Jenny wrote: *All I did was roll the dice. I placed my numbers down with what made sense. Like if I had 933 and got a six on my last roll I would put it as 60.*

Kimm wrote (see figure 1.1): *For [my] number one [game], I choose those numbers because I thought it would help me. But it didn't. What I should of done was put more hundreds than 10's*

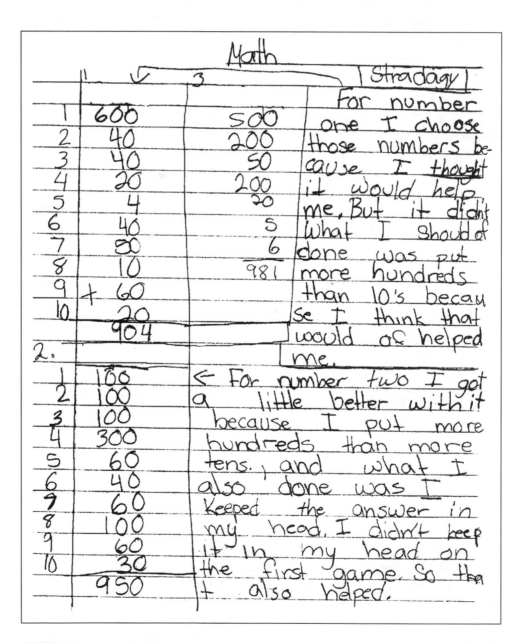

FIGURE 1.1

Kimm improved her second game because of what she learned during her first game.

because I think that would of helped me.

For [my] number two [game] I got a little better with it because I put more hundreds than more tens, and . . . keeped the answer [total] in my head. . . .

Carl wrote: *When playing Get to 1,000, I learned you have to ceep track of the numbers because you mite pass 1,000. I liked playing because I can learn how to add better. In the first game I got 970 and in the second game I got 980. In the first game I needed 30 to get to 1,000 in the second game I needed 20 to get to 1,000.*

Extending the Activity

Pam Long had taught her sixth graders Get to 1,000, and the students had been playing the game for several days before I came in to introduce several extensions. "Today I'm going to teach you how to play a few other versions of Get to 1,000," I told them. "I'd like you to play the new versions and see how they compare. In version A, you play the game using ten rolls, just like the original game, only this time, instead of multiplying the number on the die by one, ten, or 100, you get to choose from one, five, or 50."

"So it's the same as the original game except you multiply by different numbers, right?" asked Nancy.

"Yes, although in both the original game and version A you get to multiply by one," I responded. "And in all these games, the goal is still to get as close to 1,000 as you can." On the chalkboard, I wrote: *Version A: multiply by 1, 5, or 50 and roll 10 times.* "In version B, you

also roll ten times, but now you multiply the number on the die by ten, 25, or 50." I then wrote version B's directions on the chalkboard.

"That sounds harder," said Carl.

"I think that's going to be easier than the other one," Anne disagreed.

"The last version, version C, is nearly the same as the original game," I said. "You multiply the number on the die by one, ten, or 100, but you only roll the die seven times." Again, I wrote the directions for version C on the chalkboard.

Observing the Students

The students were excited about trying the variations and immediately partnered up and began playing. I was curious to see how the class would respond to the different versions. I was also interested in their strategies for winning and how they calculated mentally.

Anne and her partner were playing version B. Anne needed to multiply 5×25, and I watched as she wrote the problem on the bottom of her paper and started to use the standard method for multiplying. I stopped her. "Can you do the problem in your head?" I asked.

She thought for just a second or two, then said, "It's 125!"

"How did you get the answer so fast?" I asked.

"I thought about money, like 25 cents," she replied. "Then I knew it really fast."

Erin and Blanca were reaching for a calculator to multiply 6×50. Again, I stopped them and asked whether they could figure it out mentally. They were stuck, so I nudged them a little: "How is six times five related to six times 50?" I asked.

"Oh, it's 300!" they said together.

"How did you figure?" I asked.

"Because six times five is 30, and you add a zero and it's 300," explained Blanca.

"Why do you add a zero?" I probed. Often children know that when you multiply by ten, you add a zero and when you multiply by 100, you add two zeros, but they can't explain why. The two girls thought for a while.

Then Erin spoke up: "Because when you multiply by five, it's 30, but if you multiply by 50, then it's ten times bigger than 30 and that's 300," she explained.

Mitch and Daniel had finished a game and had added up a string of numbers on the calculator, but I noticed that the total was unreasonable. I asked them to check the answer by adding in their head. Mitch proceeded to add the 100s, then the tens, then the leftover ones, and came up with the correct answer. "It's faster to do it in my head!" he exclaimed.

Many students were surprised at how easy and fast it was to calculate mentally. One student was stuck trying to multiply 6×25 in his head. A student next to him suggested that he think of how many 25s there are in 100 and solve it that way.

Solving problems mentally helps students develop their number sense because it forces them to rely on what they know about numbers and operations. When students begin to calculate mentally rather than using standard algorithms with paper and pencil, the focus shifts from thinking about procedures to thinking about what makes sense.

A Class Discussion

The next day I led a class discussion about the game. "Raise your hand if you were able to play all three versions of Get to 1,000," I said. Nearly everyone's hand went up. "What did you think of the different versions?"

"I played A," said Michael. "It wasn't really easy to get to 1,000, because it didn't have really high numbers to multiply by. It had one, five, and 50, and the highest number you could get was 300."

"Why is that?" I asked.

"Because the highest number on the die is six, and if you multiply by 50 that's 300," Michael explained. "In the original game, you could make 600 points on one turn by multiplying six times 100."

"First, I played version C, because I thought it would be a challenge to get to 1,000 in only seven tries," Xavier began. "It *was* a challenge! I noticed that I used the 100s more in this one than I did when we had ten chances before. My strategy changed a little."

"I think version B is the hardest one to play, because you're not allowed to multiply by one," said Mitch. "When I was playing a game with

Daniel, I had 975 and it was my turn to roll. I rolled the die and I got a six. I was kind of mad, and Daniel started laughing about it because he knew he was going to win. Then I started laughing about it and I knew that the only lowest thing I could do was to multiply six by ten. That's how I lost version B."

"Any other ideas to report?" I asked.

"I found out a lot of things about multiplying," said Blanca. "It's not so hard to multiply numbers in your head."

"On C you only have seven rolls. So you use more 100s instead of tens," Jenny said. "Also, with version C, I don't think anyone uses one as a multiplier or your outcome would be too low."

"I played C with seven rolls," said Rob. "It's different from ten rolls because you need to get to 1,000 faster so you need to use bigger numbers."

"Do you think these are games of skill or games of chance?" I asked. "Talk with someone near you about this question." After a few moments, I called on Mindy.

"I think it's luck, because you never know what's going to come up on the die," she said.

"I think you need to have both luck and skill," said Jenny. "For one thing, you have to make decisions along the way. If you're close to 1,000, you have to decide what you're going to multiply the number on the die by. You have to know what's going to happen to the number on the die and how close to 1,000 you'll get. With the die, you never know what's going to happen."

"I think you can predict what's going to happen on the die," countered Carl. "I don't think you're going to roll the same number over and over. I think when you roll, you're likely to get different numbers most of the time."

"If you had to invent your own version of Get to 1,000, what directions would you use?" I asked.

"Maybe have other numbers to multiply the die by," suggested Gordon, "like maybe put some hard ones in there, like five, 15, and 30."

"I'd make it so you have more than ten rolls, say 15 rolls," said Nicole.

A Writing Assignment

When our discussion was over, I had the sixth graders write about the games (examples of their writing are shown in figures 1.2, 1.3, and 1.4). Reading their papers gave me further information about their thinking.

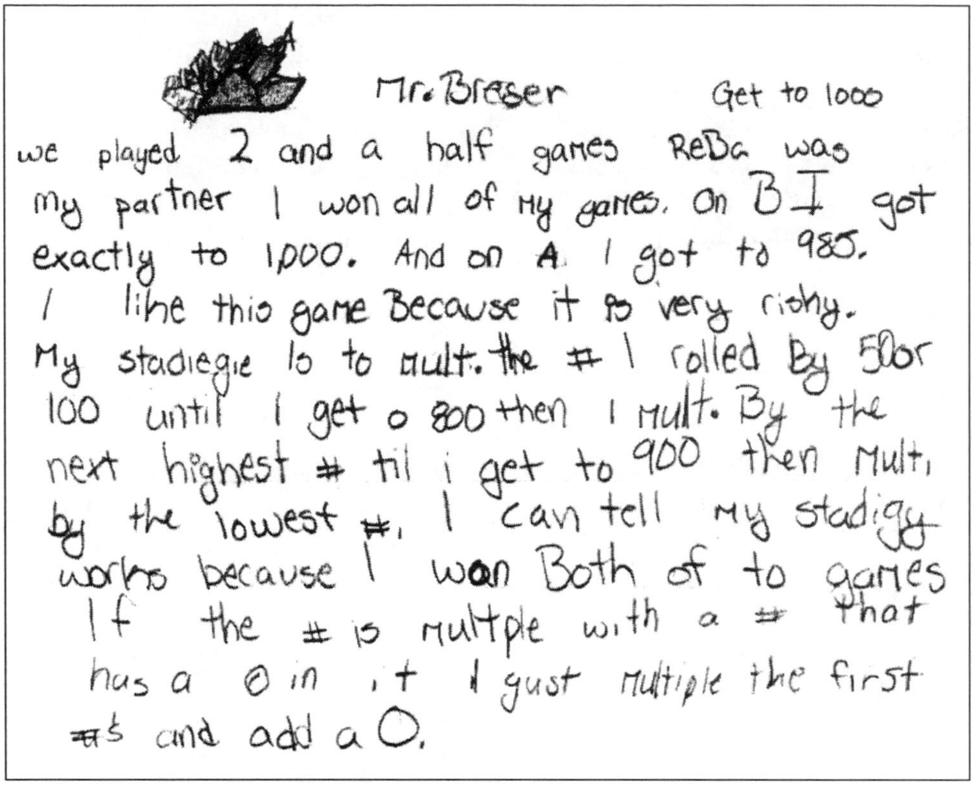

Mr. Breser   Get to 1000

we played 2 and a half games ReBa was my partner I won all of my games. On B I got exactly to 1,000. And on A. I got to 985. I like this game Because it is very risky. My stadiegie Is to mult. the # I rolled by 5 0r 100 until I get o 800 then I mult. By the next highest # til i get to 900 then Mult, by the lowest #. I can tell my stadigy works because I won Both of to games If the # is multple with a # that has a 0 in it I gust multiple the first #s and add a 0.

FIGURE 1.2

Anne realized that her strategy worked and thought the game was risky.

Get To 1000

     I think Version C was the best because
it was easy and you don't go up as high in numbers
Since you only get seven rolls you do go a lot past
100 unless you roll sixes everytime and multiply it by
one hundred. I also liked Version B because it was
a challenge to me. I knew what the answers were
when I multiplied them It was a challenge to pick the
right number to multiply it by. When I multiplied the
number I rolled by 50 all I had to do was ~~not~~ take
off the zero and multiply the number I rolled
by 5. IF I rolled a six all ~~the~~ I would have
to do is take off the zero in fifty and
multiply six by five and then just add on the
zero.

FIGURE 1.3

*Katie explained what she liked about versions
B and C.*

Get to 1,000

First I played version C becouse I thought it would be a challenge to get to 1,000 in only 7 try's. It was a challenge. I noticed that I used the hundreds more in this one than I did when we had 10 chances before. Then I played version A becouse it was different from the others becouse you could multiply by 1,5, and 50. I thought it was harder than all the others becouse it was hard to multiply by those numbers than 1,10, and 100. I didn't get to play version B but I think it would of ben harder than all the others becouse it had harder numbers to multiply by.

FIGURE 1.4

Xavier compared all the versions of Get to 1,000.

RUSTY ANSWERS YOUR QUESTIONS

What is the purpose of this activity?

In this activity, I want students to think about numbers, their magnitude, and their relationship to 1,000. I also want students to get a sense of what multiplication does to numbers. These are important characteristics of number sense.

One of the things I like about this game is that students must make decisions based on how close or how far away they are from 1,000. In other words, they must think about numbers and how those numbers relate to 1,000. For example, when I was modeling the game for Kathleen Gallagher's fourth graders, I had a score of 560 and rolled a six. I stopped to ask whether anyone had any advice for me. When Sue responded, "I think you should multiply by ten because you already have over 500, and if you multiply by 100 you'll go over 1,000, because 600 and 500 is 1,100," she was doing a number of things. In addition to multiplying and adding, she was thinking about what to do based on what would happen if I multiplied by 10 or 100. She was also thinking about how close 560 is to 1,000. Sue was reasoning about numbers, which is what students must do in order to develop their number sense.

Another focus of the activity is for students to experience and become proficient at multiplying by multiples of ten and other important landmark numbers, like 25. Because our number system is based on powers of ten, the numbers 10, 100, 1000, and their multiples are especially important landmark numbers. Landmark numbers are familiar landing places which make for simple calculations and to which other numbers can be related. In solving problems, people with well-developed number sense draw on their knowledge of these important landmarks. For example, when a sixth grader in Pam Long's class had trouble multiplying 25×6 in his head, another student suggested he think about how many 25s there are in 100 and work from there. This would also be a good strategy for solving more difficult problems, like 25×17. Knowing about 10, 100, 1,000, their multiples, and their factors is the basis of good number sense.

If I use Get to 1,000, I'll need to manage a classroom in which students are active, vocal, and working in groups. What advice do you have?

It isn't easy to manage a classroom, and in some ways it's even more challenging to manage an active one. The best-laid plans can still lead to disaster if students aren't listening and following directions.

What's most important is that you work to establish a classroom environment in which mutual respect is valued. In my classroom we have the golden rule posted, and we discuss it daily: *Treat others the way you want to be treated.* This applies to classroom discussions as well, and I'm constantly reminding children to listen to the speaker and raise a hand if they want to talk. After many years in the classroom, I'm still reminded daily that getting children to listen to one another and get along requires consistent effort.

Giving clear directions is also an important ingredient in managing a math class. Children who know what's expected of them are less likely to misbehave.

Finally, if you understand the task at hand and are aware of the goals and the important mathematical ideas of an activity, you are bound to be more confident and able to listen for clues from the children in order to move the activity from one place to another.

How can I assess a student's number sense?

When I use this activity, I have several questions in mind as I watch students play the game and as I listen to their questions and responses during class discussions.

- Are students able to multiply numbers by ten and multiples of ten? Are they able to multiply numbers by 25? by other landmark numbers?

- Do students know the effect multiplication has on numbers? Do they have a sense of how big a number will get when you multiply it by 1, 10, or 100?
- Do students have a sense of how close they are to 1,000 when they're playing the game?
- Are students using strategies to win the game? What strategies are they using?
- Are students able to keep track of their score mentally or do they use paper and pencil?
- How do students figure out the difference between their score and their partner's score? Can they figure the difference mentally?

Can I use this game in a third-grade classroom?

Yes, but instead of having 1,000 as the goal, I'd ask third graders to try to get to 100, using one through six as multipliers. What's nice about this game is that it can easily be adapted to the skill level of the players by adjusting the goal, the number of rolls of the die, and the multipliers. No matter what version of the game is played, the important thing is that students think about the effect multiplication has on numbers.

2 *Oh No! 99!*

Good Addition Practice!

Mid-: Give k... 100 chart if having difficulty

Good game to entice students

strategy involved

Overview

While older elementary students are typically engaged with larger whole numbers, many still need and benefit from practice with mental addition and subtraction of smaller numbers. In this two-person card game, players attempt to force their partner to be the one to push their jointly accumulating score above 99. The game provides practice with adding and subtracting while also giving students the chance to think strategically.

Materials Needed

A deck of playing cards (jokers removed) for each pair of students.

Card Values and Operations

Aces:	add 1
Jacks:	subtract 10
Queens:	wild cards that can represent any other card in the deck
Kings:	add zero
All others (2–10):	add their face value

Directions for Playing the Game

1. One player shuffles the cards and deals four cards to each player. The undealt cards remain in a stack, face down.

2. Players take turns playing one card at a time, adding or subtracting the value of their card to or from their jointly accumulating score.

3. Each time a player plays a card, he or she must replace it with the top card on the face-down stack.

4. Play continues until one player forces his or her partner to go over the score of 99.

IN THE CLASSROOM WITH CAREN

Introducing the Activity

To introduce Oh No! 99! to Kathleen Gallagher's fifth graders, I'd planned to go through a sample game with the whole class and then send them off to play with partners. I began by asking the class to join me in a circle on the rug, so everyone would have a good view of the deck of cards. After some adjusting of desks and bodies, we were ready to begin.

"I brought a lot of decks of cards here today because you're going to learn a card game," I announced.

"Is it poker?" asked Chip, to a round of giggles.

"No, it's not poker and it doesn't involve gambling," I replied. "It's a game you play with a partner that helps you with math. I like this game a lot. It gives you a lot of practice adding numbers in your head. It makes you think."

Set Purpose

I walked to the board and wrote *Oh No! 99!*

"This game is called Oh No! 99! As I explain the game you might start to get some ideas about how it got its name. Now before I show you how to play, there are a few important things you need to know about the cards." I wrote *A, J, Q, K* on the board. "In Oh No! 99! an ace means add one point," I explained. I wrote *add 1* next to the *A*. "A jack means subtract ten. A queen is wild. That means you can assign the queen the value of any other card in the deck."

"It can be any number?!" asked Jeannette, wide eyed.

"Can it be 1,000?" asked Kenneth.

"Well, it can't be 1,000, because there's no other card in the deck worth 1,000. It's wild, but it's not that wild," I told the class. I proceeded with my explanation. "A king means you don't add or subtract anything. For the rest of the cards in the deck, add whatever their number is: an eight means add eight, a three means add three. I'm going to leave this information up on the board, because you might need it when you play with your partner. The object of the game is to make your partner go over 99. So I want to force you to put down a card that makes the total 100 or more, and you want to try to get me to do the same. Can you guess why this game is called Oh No! 99!?" I asked.

"Because if there's 99 already, you're in trouble," offered Enrique.

"You got it," I agreed. "Before you go back to your tables, though, we're going to play one game together so you can see what the game is like and I can answer any questions. Since this is a game for partners, I'll play with the whole class as my partner. We're going to take turns adding cards to the discard pile."

I dealt four cards to myself and four cards to the class. I dealt all the cards face up, although I explained that when they played by themselves, they'd keep their cards hidden so their partner wouldn't know what they had.

"Okay, I'll go first, and I'll put down this seven. And since I put down a card, I need to pick another card from the top of the deck. I always want to have four cards in my hand. Now it's your turn. Who would like to choose a card for the class?" Many hands shot up. I called on Greg.

"I'll use the nine," Greg announced.

I put the nine on top of the seven.

"So now what's the total for the pile?" I asked the class.

"Sixteen!" they responded in unison.

"Good," I said, "whenever you put a card down on the pile you have to tell what the new total is. Partners need to check each other and pay attention to make sure both of you know the total."

We continued playing. I called on various students to make a choice for the class, and had the whole class tell me the new total after each card was added. When the total of the pile was 88, I asked Jenny to choose a card for the class to play. Many students tried to influence her.

"Don't use the ace yet," advised Miguel.

"Put down the nine," suggested Annabel.

Realizing the advice was being motivated by strategic thinking, I stopped the game to point this out: "I'm noticing that many of you have ideas about which card to play next. Would anyone like to explain your thinking?" I called on Kate.

"I think we should save the ace."

"Why is that?" I asked.

"Because with an ace you only have to add one, and that's a low number. If the cards get up to a high number like 97 or 98, we can use the ace to make you go over 99."

Many students nodded in agreement.

"Okay," I continued, "Kate thinks you should hold onto your ace and save it for later. Does anyone have an idea about which card you might want to play next?"

"Use the nine," said Ana, "because then the total will be 97 and that's close to 99. If you don't have a low card or a jack, queen, or king, we could win."

The class played the nine, and my next play put the score over 99. I then sent the students off to their tables to play the game in pairs. "Remember," I told them, "this game is important for two reasons. First, it gives you a lot of practice adding in your head. Second, when the total gets close to 99, you have to do a lot of thinking to plan a good strategy."

Observing the Students

The students returned to their seats, and I circulated around the room. At first, I just wanted to make sure everyone understood the game and was playing with a partner. Then I spent some time observing individual games. Several students were quite animated and couldn't resist showing their cards to friends nearby. Miguel, for one, was proudly flashing his picture cards to anyone in his vicinity. I issued a few gentle reminders for students to stay in their seats and focus on the game.

I noticed that while many students were quickly and easily calculating the totals mentally, others were more hesitant; some were even using their fingers. I was surprised to see Chip use his fingers to add 10 to 43. Adding ten should come automatically to most fifth graders, especially one like Chip, who came from a very traditional math program. However, it was clear that he had not made the base ten connection in this context. While Chip was certainly capable of adding 10 and 43 on paper using the standard algorithm, he did not see the significance of the relationship between the two numbers nor that there was a very predictable pattern when adding ten.

A Writing Assignment

After about fifteen minutes, even though everyone was still very involved in playing the game, I called everyone back together. I wanted to see what kinds of strategies they were using at this point, and I wanted them to have the opportunity to hear some of their classmates' thinking about the game so far. I illustrated a hypothetical situation on a projected transparency.

"Imagine," I said, "that you're playing Oh No! 99! and the total is up to 87. Your four cards are a six, a queen, an ace, and a king. Which card would you play next? As you think about this, pay attention to why you're choosing a particular card. I'm going to give you ten minutes of quiet writing time so you can tell me your ideas on this question. Make sure you put your name and date on the paper. Are there any questions?"

"You just want us to tell you which card we would use?" asked Jon.

"That's part of it," I answered, "but I also want to know why you would choose that card instead of any of the others. You might even want to tell me which card you definitely *wouldn't* want to use and why."

Most students chose either the six or the queen as their next card on the pile. Traci wrote, *I would put the 6 down because you should get rid of your high cards and save your low cards as you get in the high 80s and 90s. A, Q, K, are not high cards because a Q is a wild card and you can use it as a K. A K is a 0. An A is a 1.* Neal made a convincing argument for the queen (see figure 2.1): *I would put down the queen as a ten so the total would be 97. 97 is a high number and if your partner has only numbers higher than four you win. If they have numbers less than four or a king, queen, jack, or ace and they lay down a queen as a two or a two, you can put down the king.*

After reading through the class papers (additional examples are shown in figures 2.2 and 2.3), I realized the question didn't dig deeply enough into the methods the students used for adding the numbers. I got a general feel for their thinking about the cards, but the prompt I used focused more on strategy. I wanted to ask a question about the game that encouraged the children to tell me more explicitly how they were combining numbers. Did they use what they knew about place value to help? Were they merely counting on? Did they have more than one way to add numbers? I decided I would try to focus on these questions next time.

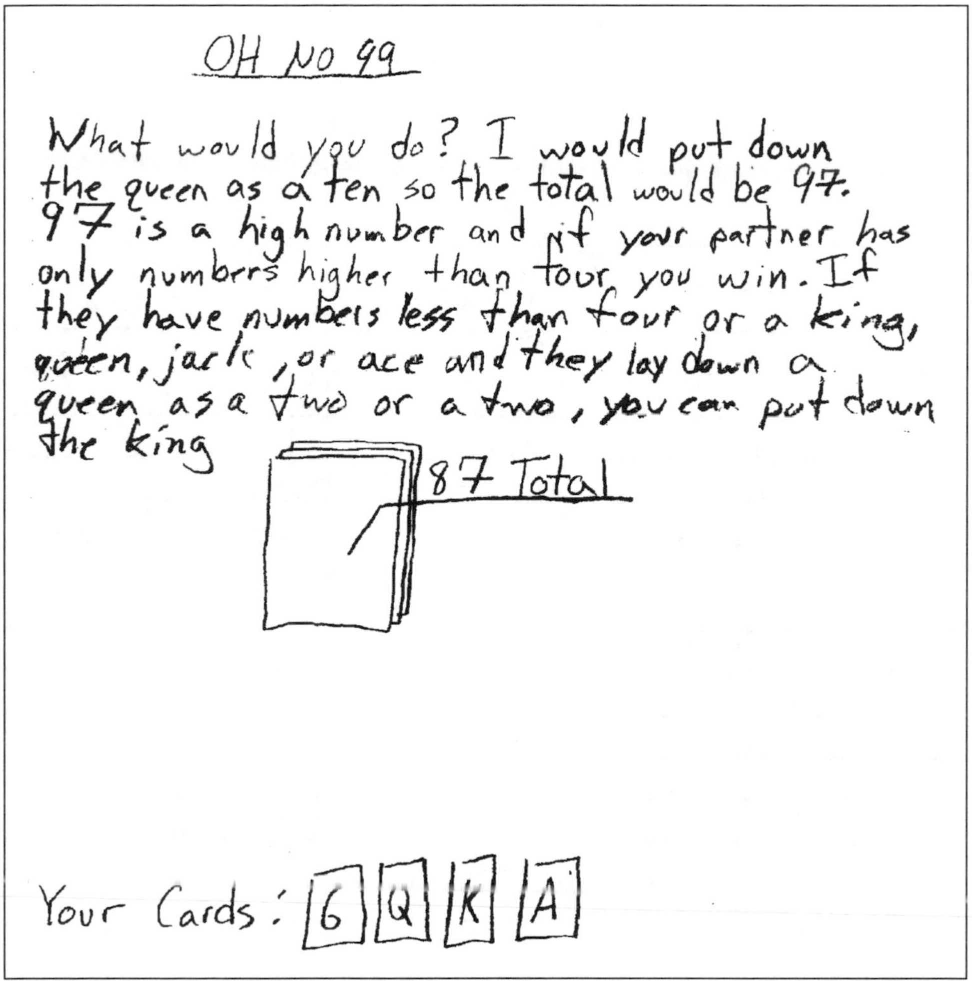

OH NO 99

What would you do? I would put down the queen as a ten so the total would be 97. 97 is a high number and if your partner has only numbers higher than four you win. If they have numbers less than four or a king, queen, jack, or ace and they lay down a queen as a two or a two, you can put down the king

87 Total

Your Cards: 6 Q K A

FIGURE 2.1

Neal's hypothetical strategy.

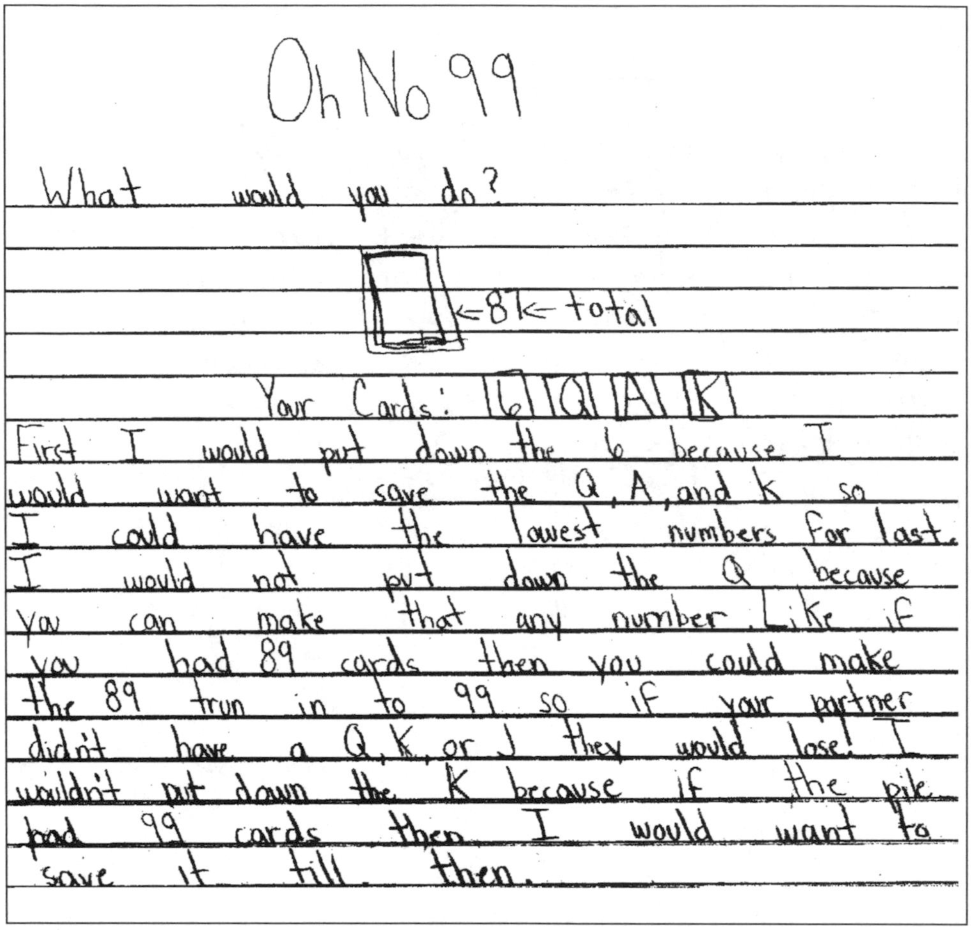

Oh No 99

What would you do?

⟵8k⟵ total

Your Cards: |6||Q||A||K|

First I would put down the 6 because I would want to save the Q, A, and K so I could have the lowest numbers for last. I would not put down the Q because you can make that any number. Like if you had 89 cards then you could make the 89 trun in to 99 so if your partner did'nt have a Q, K, or J they would lose! I wouldn't put down the K because if the pile had 99 cards then I would want to save it till then.

FIGURE 2.2
Another student's strategy.

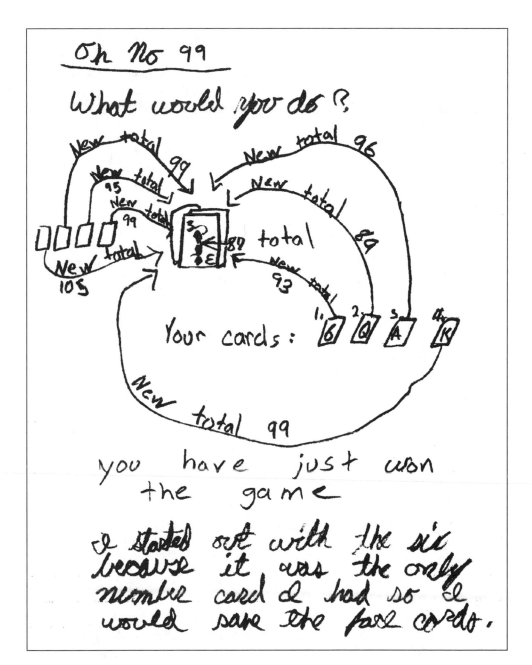

you have just won
the game

I started out with the six
because it was the only
number card I had so I
would save the face cards.

FIGURE 2.3
Still another strategy.

Continuing the Activity

When I returned to the class a few days later, student partners were playing the game with gusto. I gave them a few minutes to finish, and then I called for their attention. I began by talking about the papers they'd written during my previous visit. I told them I was impressed with both the range of their ideas and the way they were able to write about their thinking.

"The last time I visited I gave you a situation to think about. Does anyone remember what the total was for the question I asked?"

"It was 87," replied Charles.

I wrote *87* on a projected transparency.

"And the cards we had were six, ace, queen, king," added Lucy.

"Okay," I continued, "quite a few of you wrote that you would use the six and add it to the pile." I wrote *+ 6* next to the *87* on the overhead. "So what would the total be now?"

"Ninety-three!"

I wrote *= 93* on the overhead to complete the equation. "Now comes the interesting part," I told the class. "You all know that 87 plus six equals 93, so that's not really a problem. The challenging part is to think about how you solved the problem in your head without paper and pencil. Does anyone want to try to describe how you solved it mentally?"

Traci volunteered first. "I took two away from the 87 to make it 85. Then I took one away from the six to make it five. I know 85 plus five equals 90.

Then I just added back the two and the one and I got 93." As Traci talked through her thinking, I recorded the corresponding equations on the overhead:

$$87 - 2 = 85$$
$$6 - 1 = 5$$
$$85 + 5 = 90$$
$$2 + 1 = 3$$
$$90 + 3 = 93$$

It's important for students to see the connections between their thinking and the mathematical symbols that represent it. Often children don't realize that the words and ideas come first and that the equation is a shorter way to express those same ideas. Many children only see equations printed in textbooks and worksheets and don't connect them with any real-world context. As a teacher, part of my job is to help students connect equations and symbols with meaningful contexts. It's a challenge to listen to a student, try to make sense of her thinking, and record the corresponding equations all at the same time, but it's gotten easier with practice.

I asked the students to volunteer other approaches to solving 87 + 6. While the problem itself is not particularly challenging for fifth graders, explaining it verbally is. I wanted the students to focus on their own thinking without getting bogged down by the computation.

Ronald shared his strategy next. "Well, I know three plus three is six. So I took one of the threes and added it to 87. That made 90. Then I added the other three to the 90 and got 93." I recorded Ronald's thinking symbolically:

$$6 = 3 + 3$$
$$87 + 3 = 90$$
$$90 + 3 = 93$$

Then I recorded Jenny's, Josue's, and Enrique's thinking on the overhead as well. The class got to hear five different students talk about their thinking and were able to see there is more than one way to solve a problem. This idea is a big leap for students who have been accustomed to an algorithmic approach to mathematics. The more opportunities they have to expand their computational horizons, the better.

A Writing Assignment

Next I wanted each student in the class to have an opportunity to explain her or his thinking about computation. I chose a similar context. "Imagine you're playing a game of Oh No! 99! and the total score so far is 74." I wrote *74* on a projected transparency. "Your partner adds an eight to the pile." I wrote *+ 8* next to the *74*. "What's the new total?"

"Eighty-two," the class responded in unison.

"Okay," I told them, "now for the challenging part. I'm going to give each of you a piece of paper and on that paper you need to try to explain different ways you can add 74 plus eight." I put the previous overhead back up to remind students of our

previous discussion. "We saw five different ways people solved the problem 87 plus six. Your job is to try to think of a lot of different ways to solve 74 plus eight. Maybe if you look at the ideas that Traci, Ronald, Jenny, Josue, and Enrique had it might help you. Probably there are even more ways to solve these kinds of problems."

"How many ways are we supposed to get?" asked Cornelius.

"I don't have a specific number in mind," I told him. "Just try to stretch your brain to think of a lot of different ideas."

I handed out paper and the students began their work. I circulated and observed. There was quite a range of approaches. I noticed that several of the students were writing prolifically and not using symbols. While I was pleased that they were comfortable incorporating writing into their math work, I decided to steer them in a different direction.

"I'm sorry to interrupt you in the middle of your work," I told the class, "but I'm noticing that some of you are doing a lot of writing. It's great to write and use words to explain your thinking, but you can also use shortcuts and write some equations on your paper." I referred once again to the transparency with the five students' work. "You see I used equations to show how Traci took two from 87 to get 85. Probably on your papers there will be a combination of words and equations to show how you solved the problem. Don't feel that you need to use only words for this assignment."

The students resumed working. I

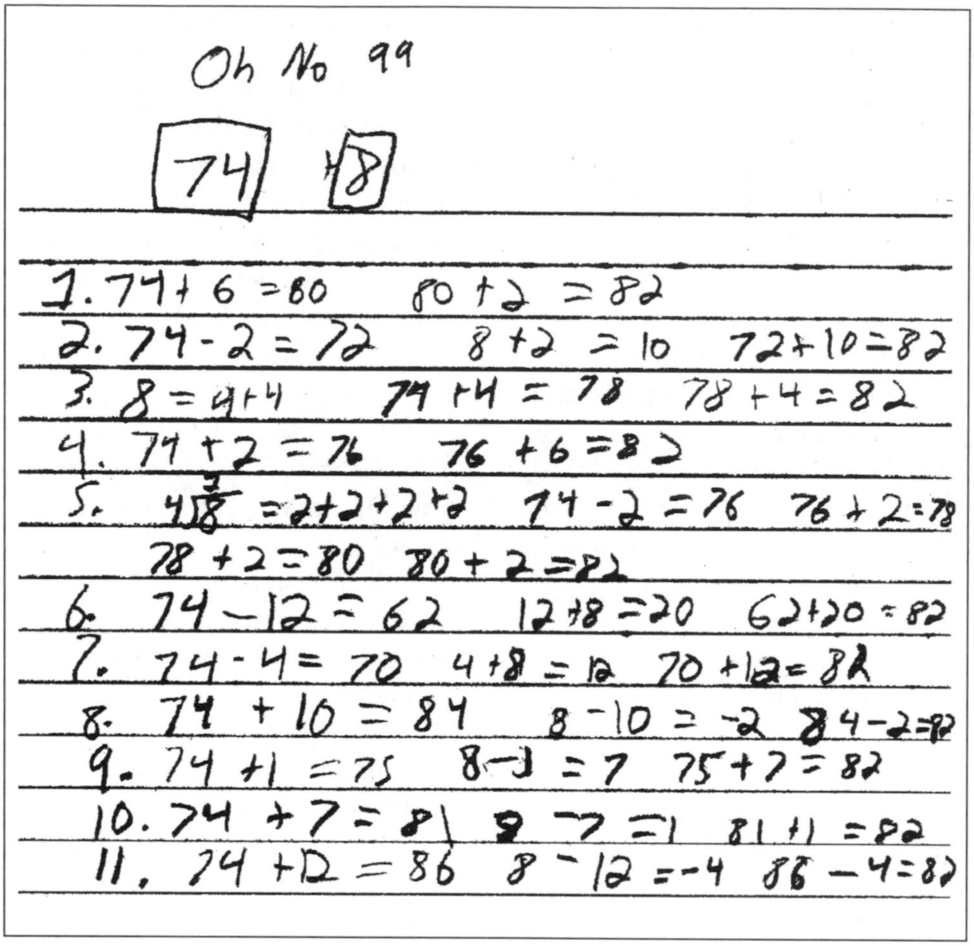

Oh No 99

74 8

1. 74 + 6 = 80   80 + 2 = 82
2. 74 - 2 = 72   8 + 2 = 10   72 + 10 = 82
3. 8 = 4 + 4   74 + 4 = 78   78 + 4 = 82
4. 74 + 2 = 76   76 + 6 = 82
5. 8 = 2 + 2 + 2 + 2   74 - 2 = 76   76 + 2 = 78
   78 + 2 = 80   80 + 2 = 82
6. 74 - 12 = 62   12 + 8 = 20   62 + 20 = 82
7. 74 - 4 = 70   4 + 8 = 12   70 + 12 = 82
8. 74 + 10 = 84   8 - 10 = -2   84 - 2 = 82
9. 74 + 1 = 75   8 - 1 = 7   75 + 7 = 82
10. 74 + 7 = 81   8 - 7 = 1   81 + 1 = 82
11. 74 + 12 = 86   8 - 12 = -4   86 - 4 = 82

FIGURE 2.4

Shannon discovered eleven ways to add 74 and 8.

sat down briefly at different tables, watching students work and occasionally asking them a question about their paper. Several students described counting on as their strategy of choice. Romolo wrote, *This is how I did the adding. I add the number 8 into the pile. I just counted 74 and then I said 75, 76, 77, 78, 79, 80, 81, 82.* He had not recorded any other strategies. Kate had two ideas: *1. I knew the answer by counting on my fingers. 2. I added [standard algorithm with carrying].*

Shannon was clearly comfortable breaking the numbers apart and putting them back together. He had listed 11 different ways to do so (see figure 2.4). Jenny used an impressive combination of words and equations to explain her thinking (see figure 2.5): *74 – 4 = 70 then 8 + 4 = 12 then*

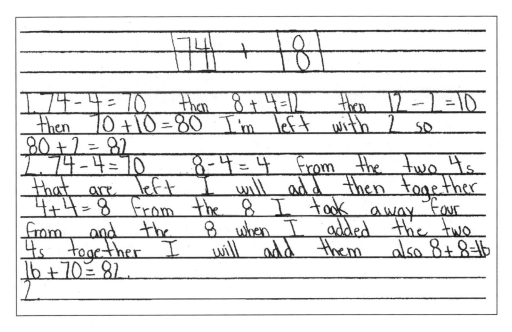

FIGURE 2.5
Jenny's ways to add 74 and 8.

12 − 2 = 10 then 70 + 10 = 80 I'm left with 2 so 80 + 2 = 82.

Jon used ten as a friendly number: *74 + 10 = 84 − 2 + 82. You − the 2 because you added 2 to the 8 and that equals 10.* I was pleased to see that quite a few of the students used division to describe breaking the eight into twos or fours. Mike wrote: *8 ÷ 2 = 4 ÷ 2 = 2, 74 + 2 = 76 + 2 = 78 + 2 = 80 + 2 = 82.*

I got the feeling some of the students were humoring me. They listed different ways to make 82, but didn't seem concerned with using the original numbers. Josue had a list that included: *60 + 22 = 82, 71 + 9 = 80 + 2 = 82.* It seemed Josue was showing what he knew about 82

rather than showing ways he might combine 74 + 8. One of Jon's contributions was: *74 ÷ 2 = 37 + 45 = 82.* I wasn't particularly concerned by these types of equations. While the original context seemed to have been lost, I was at least able to see some different ways the boys thought about numbers.

However, I found some of the written work very confusing. Annabel wrote: *70 − 4 = 70, 4 + 2 = 6, 76 + 7 = 82.* Not only was it unclear where the numbers had come from, the work also had computational errors. I would need to get back to Annabel one on one and have her explain her work to me. The paper alone left me with questions about her thinking.

A Class Discussion

After the students had been working independently for a while, I stopped the class and had them share their work in groups. Each student showed a way he or she had solved the problem. Then I called the class together to summarize the experience. "Does anyone have any comments about this activity?" I asked.

"I like the game," responded Miguel, "but it's hard to write about adding the numbers."

"I got eight different ways to add them," bragged Howard. "Probably I could find more."

"Why do you think I asked you to write so much about 74 plus eight?" I asked.

"Because you're the math teacher," quipped Ana.

"Well that's certainly part of it," I laughed, "but why did I ask you this particular math question?"

"It makes us think a lot," responded Kenneth.

"So you can see our ideas," added Enrique.

"You know," I said, "I think that's really it. I try to ask questions that get you to think. And I want to be able to understand your thinking so I can be a better teacher."

CAREN ANSWERS YOUR QUESTIONS

What is the purpose of this activity?

Oh No! 99! provides a context in which students can practice mental computation. During the game, the students are repeatedly adding and occasionally subtracting numbers between 1 and 99. This certainly gives them the practice they need to become computationally proficient and efficient.

Additionally, the game motivates students. Whereas they might be less than thrilled to do dozens of computation problems with no context, they actually choose to play Oh No! 99! Even after playing it several times in class, students still enjoy the game and are eager to play it during menu or choice time.

Then too, the game gives students an opportunity to use strategic thinking while they are playing. Students need to consider the value of the cards in their hand, hypothesize about what cards their partners might have, and make decisions based on their ideas.

Finally, the game provides a context in which students can do some written work. Their writing gives insights into how they communicate mathematically and how they think about breaking numbers apart and putting numbers together. It's important for students to have many opportunities to practice these skills.

Is this game too easy for fifth graders?

On the surface this is an easy game, but there is a lot of mathematics embedded in it. Students playing Oh No! 99! are practicing mental computation, using strategic thinking, and being exposed to probability. One test of the game is how interested the students are. If it were truly too easy, the students would lose interest rather quickly. How long would a group of fifth graders stay involved in a preschool puzzle or an episode of *Sesame Street*? In Kathleen Gallagher's class students continued to choose to play Oh No! 99! during their free time throughout the year.

Also, I noticed several of the fifth graders using their fingers to figure the totals during the game. This suggests they need much more practice with mental computation. While I don't forbid students to count on their fingers, I work with them to help them move on to more efficient strategies. The game, when combined with a discussion about computation strategies, offers the students opportunities to move beyond "counting on" approaches. The game also develops number sense in students who do not rely on their fingers. The strategies they learn and fortify while playing can be applied to larger, more challenging problems in the future.

What can I learn about my students from this game?

I found many opportunities to assess individual students while they were playing. By observing them and listening to their conversations I got a feel for their comfort with the computation and the ways they were adding in their head. The writing prompt I used gave me deeper insight into their strategic thinking. Also, the game proved to be an excellent springboard for a discussion about mental computation strategies and

ways to put numbers together and take them apart. Such flexible thinking about numbers strengthens students' number sense.

During the game Chip had trouble mentally adding 10 to 43. As I watched him play the game with his partner, I saw he was clearly embarrassed and attempted to hide his finger counting and acted silly to distract his partner and me from his struggle. By the intermediate grades, students are painfully aware of their academic shortcomings and in some cases have become quite adept at hiding them. This is true not only in math, but in all areas. So a big part of my role as the teacher is to assess students informally. Observations, interviews, and student work really give me the big picture. When I do notice a student, like Chip, who is "sneaking by" without real understanding, I need to provide a safe environment for him to have more meaningful experiences with numbers.

What experiences would you provide for a student like Chip?

Chip definitely needs more opportunities to work with numbers in ways that make sense to him. The rote drills and algorithms he learned in the past did not serve him well when it came to doing even simple computation. I need to ask Chip questions about patterns he notices in numbers. This may help him begin to see the reason in our place value system. Perhaps a 1–100 chart will give him a visual model of our number system. He and his partner can use the

100 chart as a game board and move a marker along the chart as the total changes with each turn. I may also have Chip keep a record of the score by writing equations horizontally on a piece of paper. For example, if the total were 58 and Chip put a seven down, he'd write *58 + 7 = 65*. Writing the equations horizontally will help keep Chip from falling into the mindless algorithm trap. He'll be more apt to think about the numbers as quantities rather than digits to cross out mechanically.

3 *Get to Zero*

Overview

This activity gives students—individually, in pairs, or in small groups—practice with adding, subtracting, multiplying, and dividing whole numbers. Students can perform the calculations mentally or use a calculator, whichever you feel is more appropriate. Players start with a three-digit number and use any series of mathematical operations involving the numbers 1 through 9 to get to zero in as few turns as possible.

Materials Needed

A calculator for each student or pair or group of students.

Directions for Playing the Game

1. Players choose a three-digit number (example: 500).

2. Players choose an initial operation and number (example: divide 500 by 5); any number from 1 to 9 and any operation can be used. *Only whole numbers are allowed! If an operation results in a decimal answer, players must go back and try another number and/or operation.*

3. Players perform the calculation mentally or on the calculator and record the result on paper (example: 500 ÷ 5 = 100) so they can look back over their work.

4. Players repeat steps 2 and 3 until they get to zero.

Sample Game Scenarios

Turn 1: 500 ÷ 5 = 100
Turn 2: 100 ÷ 5 = 20

Turn 3: 20 ÷ 5 = 4
Turn 4:   4 − 4 = 0

Turn 1: 752 ÷ 4 = 188
Turn 2: 188 ÷ 2 = 94
Turn 3: 94 − 4 = 90
Turn 4: 90 ÷ 9 = 10
Turn 5: 10 ÷ 5 = 2
Turn 6:   2 − 2 = 0

Extensions

1. Give everyone the same number to start with and challenge the class to get to zero in as few operations as possible.

2. Ask students to find as many three-step numbers (those from which you can get to zero in only three operations) as they can.

IN THE CLASSROOM WITH RUSTY

Introducing the Activity

"I'm going to teach you an activity called Get to Zero," I began. "You'll need a calculator and a piece of paper and a pencil. You may work alone, with a partner, or with a small group."

The sixth graders in Pam Long's class had each been assigned a calculator the first week of school, and everyone now eagerly pulled it from his or her desk. To help model the directions, I used Pam's overhead calculator, as well as a projected transparency on which I could record numbers.

"To begin, you need to choose any three-digit number," I explained. "Once you've chosen your number, write it down on your paper. Would anyone like to suggest a three-digit number for us to work on together?"

"How about 500," offered Nancy.

I wrote *500* on the transparency. "Our goal is to get to zero in as few mathematical operations as possible," I said. "You may use any operation: addition, subtraction, multiplication, or division. When using one of those operations, you may only use the numbers one through nine. I'll work through an example. What operation should we begin with?"

"I think you should start with division because it gets you a smaller number than all the other operations," said Carl. Students nodded their head in agreement. Although Carl's idea was

obvious to these sixth graders, the comment signaled a sense of numbers and operations.

I then proposed dividing 500 by five. I chose the number five because I knew it wouldn't yield an answer with a remainder. I wanted to keep things uncomplicated while modeling the activity.

"I'll begin by dividing 500 by five," I stated. "What's 500 divided by five?"

"One hundred!" the students chorused.

Then I punched the numbers into the overhead calculator, encouraging students to verify the answers using the calculators at their tables. Calculating mentally not only often is faster than a calculator and makes more sense but also helps develop mathematical thinking.

I wrote *divide by 5* under the number *500* on the transparency before I continued. This was turn number one.

"Now I'll divide by five again," I told them. "I want you to mentally divide 100 by five."

After a few moments, several students raised their hand. I asked the class quietly to say the answer to 100 divided by five. Then we verified the answer on the calculator to be sure it was 20. Again, I wrote *divide by 5* for turn number two.

"Now we have 20 showing on the calculator," I said. "We want to get to zero in as few moves as possible, so what should we do?"

"Divide by five again!" exclaimed Manuel.

"Or divide by four," added Mary.

"What about divide by ten?" asked Michael.

"That wouldn't work, you can only use one through nine," said Todd, reminding Michael of the rules.

"Think about what would get us the smallest quotient, or answer," I suggested. After a few seconds, several hands flew up. I called on Carl.

"If you divide 20 by five you'll get four, but if you divide it by four you'll get five," he said. "So I think we should divide by five."

"I don't think it matters," Gordon interjected. "Because either way you'll get to zero in the same number of turns."

"Gordon, can you tell us more about that?" I asked.

"Well, if you divide 20 by five, the answer's four and then you could subtract four to get to zero," he explained. "If you divide 20 by four you get five and all you have to do is subtract five to get to zero. For both, you get to zero in two turns."

"Does that make sense?" I asked. Students nodded their head.

"We could choose four or five as a divisor," I said. "Let's try five and divide 20 by five."

"It's four," said Hannah.

"Okay," I responded. "In this game, it's handy to use the calculator to keep track of what's happening to the numbers as we make our way to zero." After I verified the answer on the calculator, I wrote *divide by 5* for turn number three. "What should we do next?" I asked.

"Subtract four!" several students chimed in.

I finished by writing *subtract 4* for turn number four. "So it took us four turns to get to zero," I said. "Let's try another one. Raise your hand if you have another three-digit number less than 1,000 for us to begin with."

"Let's start with an odd number," suggested Blanca. Blanca often challenged the group and she exuded confidence when working with numbers. "How about 123?"

I wrote *123* on a new transparency. "I want you to talk with your neighbor about what operation and number we should use to begin," I said. After a moment, I asked for volunteers and called on Xavier.

"Divide 123 by two," he suggested.

Several students groaned and others shook their head in disagreement.

"Before we divide 123 by two, I'm interested in hearing what you think will happen," I said.

"I think the answer is going to be a number with a remainder," Cam predicted.

"Why do you think that?" I asked.

"Because two will go into 12 evenly, but two won't go into three evenly," he responded. Cam appeared to be solving 123 divided by two using the long-division algorithm.

"I think you won't end up with a whole number and you have to have a whole number for an answer or else it's really hard to get to zero," said Jenny.

"When you're dividing, how do you know if you'll get an answer that's a whole number?" I asked.

"You just have to have the feeling for what's going to divide evenly into a number," Kerry mused. "If you don't know, then you'd have to play around with the numbers until you get a whole number."

"Let's use our calculators and divide 123 by two," I instructed. Students soon realized that dividing by two resulted in an answer with a remainder.

"I got 61.5," Cam reported. "That's the same as 61 and a half. If you get a decimal, it's hard to get to zero."

"So it's important that you end up with a whole number for an answer whether you divide, multiply, subtract, or add. I think Xavier's idea helped us learn new things about this activity," I said. "How about another idea?"

"Let's divide 123 by three," offered Hannah. "I'm picking divide

by three because 123 is a multiple of three."

Students used their calculators to divide and came up with 41 as an answer. I continued to keep track of the operations and numbers we were using on the projected transparency, modeling for students how they might keep track of their decisions. (Figure 3.1 shows how Niqueta kept track of her games.)

"What next?" I asked.

"We should subtract one so we get to an even number," said Devin. "That would give us 40."

I wrote *subtract 1* on the transparency. That was our second operation. I asked students to think about what to do next and reminded them that we wanted to get to zero in

346	300	600	800	900	1,000	160
$\frac{0}{0}$ 2	÷2	÷2	÷2	÷2	÷2	÷2
-9	÷2	÷2	÷5	÷2	÷5	÷2
-9	÷2	÷2	÷5	÷5	÷4	÷5
-7	÷2	÷5	-9	÷5	÷5	-5
÷2	-9	-9	-7	-9	-5	
÷2	-9	-6	343	1000		
÷2	200	729	512	÷7	÷10	
950	÷5	÷9	÷8	÷7	÷10	
÷2	÷5	÷9	÷8	-7	-10	
÷5	-8	-9	-8			
÷5						
-9						
-1						
-9						

FIGURE 3.1
Niqueta's record of her Get to Zero games.

as few operations as possible. Someone suggested dividing 40 by two, but that idea was vetoed in favor of dividing by five. Students were beginning to make sense of the game. We divided 40 by five to get eight, then subtracted eight to get to zero in four turns.

Observing the Students

After we finished this second game together, students got to work; some partnered up and some worked alone. The game was motivating and sustained the students' interest. I moved around the room, mostly observing and asking questions.

I noticed that being able to use the calculators freed the students to explore numbers and operations. They seemed uninhibited and challenged by trying to get to zero in as few operations as possible.

A Writing Assignment

After about twenty-five minutes, when it seemed that most students had explored several sequences, I asked them to write about the game. I provided these prompts:

- This game helps me learn . . .
- I discovered . . .
- I think . . .
- I found out . . .

A Class Discussion

After giving students about ten minutes to write, I called the group back together for a class discussion. "Raise your hand if you'd like to tell us about something you discovered," I said.

"The fastest way to get to zero is by using division," reported Katie.

"If you're like at 443 or something, you want to subtract to have your number end in zero, so you can divide by five easily," said Anne.

"Tell us more about that, Anne," I probed.

"Well, if you're at 443 and you subtract three you get to 440 and you can then divide by five evenly, because I know that numbers that end in zero are multiples of five," she explained.

"What else did you discover?" I continued.

"That, like 555, 444, 333, all come out the same way," said Carl.

"Give us an example, and I'll write the numbers on the chalkboard," I told him. "Everyone else use your calculator and follow along with us."

"Five hundred and fifty-five divided by five equals 111, divide by three equals 37, subtract seven equals 30, divide by six equals five, subtract five equals zero," he reported. "It works for every three-digit number where the digits are all the same. You get to zero in five turns." (Carl's written work is shown in figure 3.2.)

"Let's try another one," I said. "Let's test Carl's conjecture."

"Four hundred and forty-four divided by four equals 111, divide by three equals 37, subtract seven equals 30, divide by six equals five, subtract five equals zero," he said carefully. The

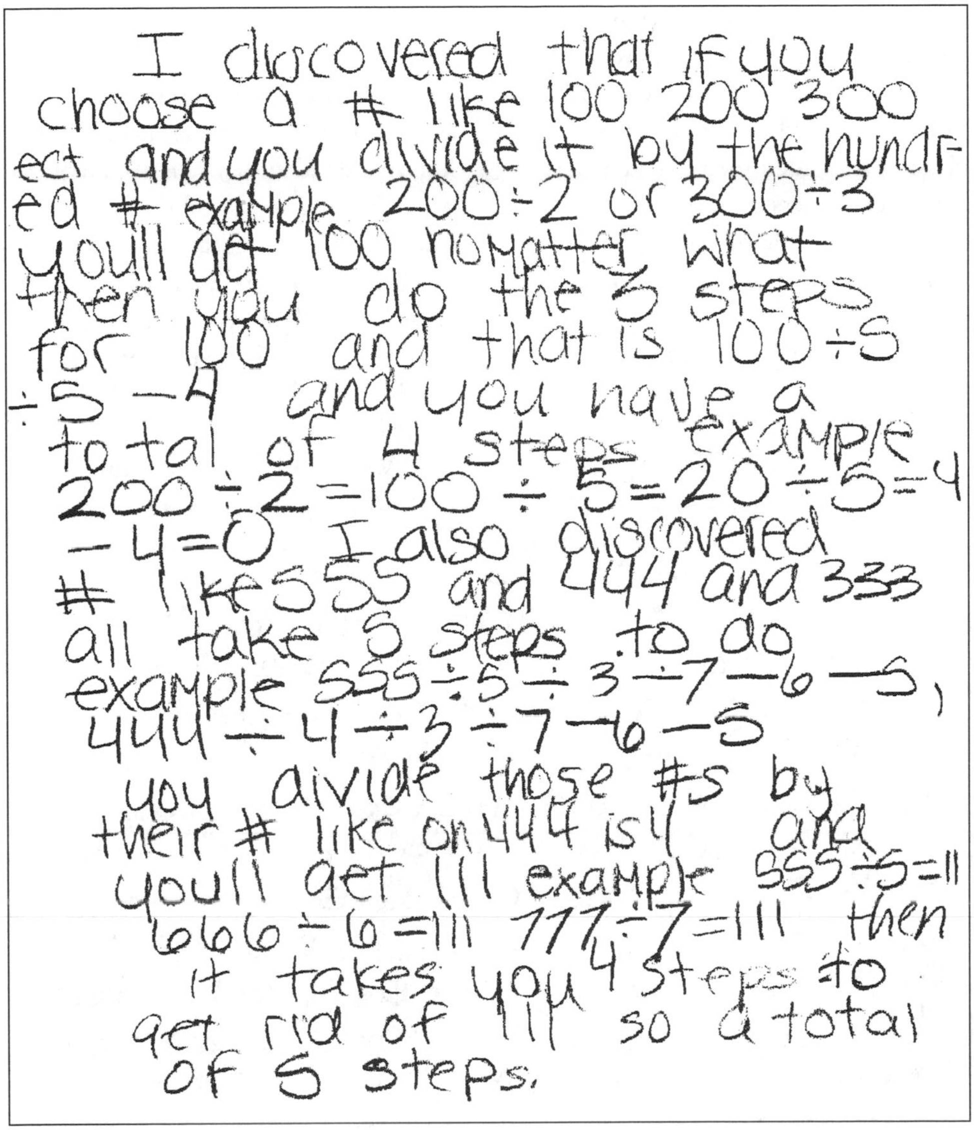

I discovered that if you choose a # like 100 200 300 ect and you divide it by the hundred # example 200÷2 or 300÷3 youll get 100 nomatter what then you do the 5 steps for 100 and that is 100÷5 ÷5 —4 and you have a total of 4 steps example 200÷2=100 ÷5=20÷5=4 —4=0 I also discovered # like 555 and 444 and 333 all take 5 steps to do example 555÷5÷3÷7—6—5, 444÷4÷3÷7—6—5 you divide those #s by their # like on 444 is 4 and youll get 111 example 555÷5=11 666÷6=111 777÷7=111 then it takes you 4 steps to get rid of 111 so a total of 5 steps.

FIGURE 3.2

Carl discovered a pattern with certain numbers.

class seemed impressed by this discovery.

"Any other discoveries?" I asked. Lots of hands shot up. I was pleased that this activity had stimulated so much thinking.

"I learned that if you have a hundred number, if you divide it by the number in the hundred's place, then you will always get 100," said Katie. "Like 800 divided by eight equals 100, 900 divided by nine equals 100, like that. I think that's important, because when you get to 100, you can get to zero in three turns." (Katie's written work is shown in figure 3.3.)

"Remember when we got to 100 in three turns when we played as a class?" I reminded them. "Did anyone get to zero in less than three turns?"

"If you divide by two digits, you could," said Anne. "But we can't do that."

"Did anyone else get to zero in three moves?" I asked.

"I got to zero in three moves starting with 200," Hannah reported. I wrote the equations on the chalkboard as she read them from her paper. "Two hundred divided by five is 40. Divide 40 by five and that's eight, then subtract eight," she read.

"How about 512," said Denny. "Five hundred and twelve divided by eight equals 64, 64 divided by eight equals eight, then subtract eight."

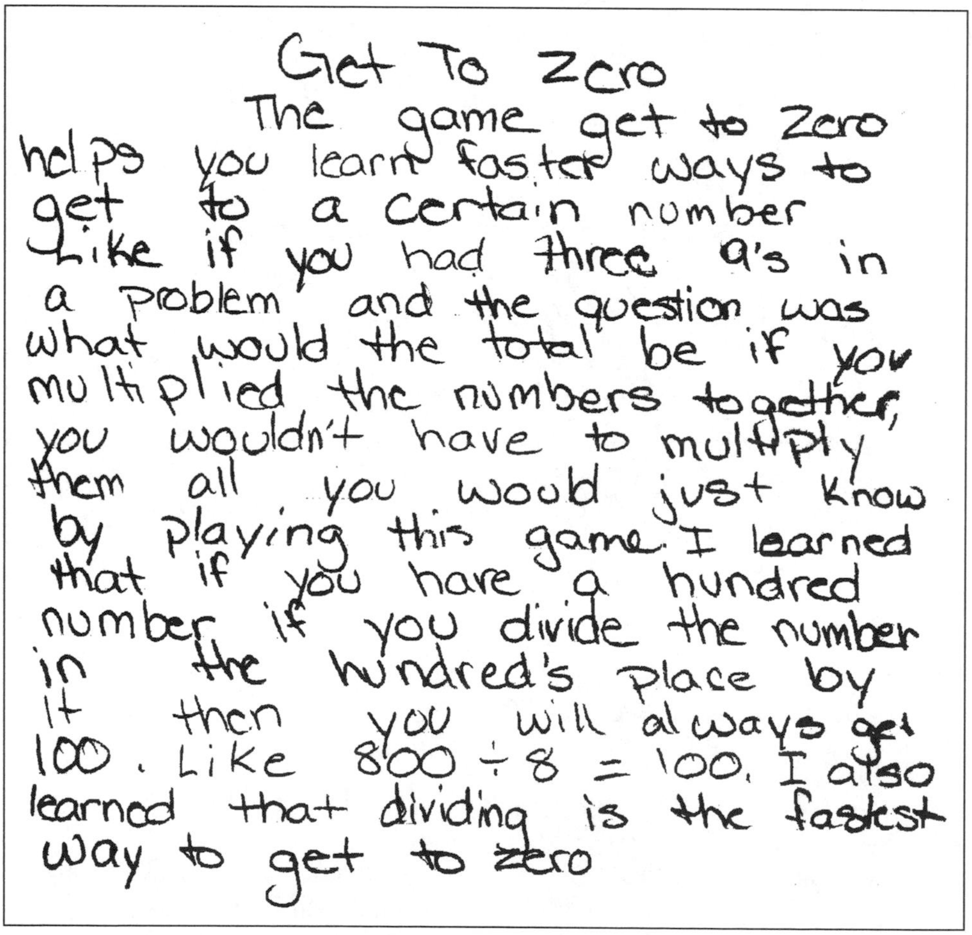
Get To Zero

The game get to Zero helps you learn faster ways to get to a certain number Like if you had three 9's in a problem and the question was what would the total be if you multiplied the numbers together, you wouldn't have to multiply them all you would just know by playing this game. I learned that if you have a hundred number if you divide the number in the hundred's place by it then you will always get 100. Like 800 ÷ 8 = 100. I also learned that dividing is the fastest way to get to zero

FIGURE 3.3

Katie realized that dividing is the fastest way to get to zero. She also discovered how to get to 100 quickly.

"Did anyone get to zero in less than three moves?" I asked. No one raised a hand.

"I think it's impossible," was Jeremy's conjecture.

"What's the largest number we can start with and get to zero in three moves?" I asked. Jenny was waving her hand so hard I thought it was going to fly off. She was smiling excitedly.

"I got 729!" she exclaimed. "I worked backwards. I multiplied nine times nine times nine and that's 729. I multiplied by nine because that's the highest number you can use with the operations. When you start with 729, you divide by nine and that equals 81. Divide 81 by nine and that's nine, then subtract nine." (Jenny's written work is shown in figure 3.4.)

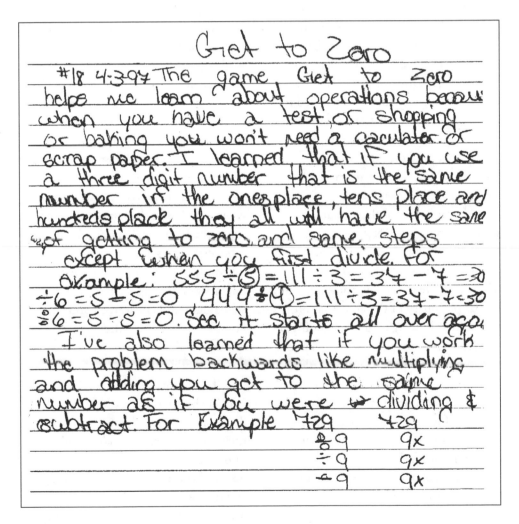

FIGURE 3.4

Jenny noticed that Get to Zero helped her learn more about operations. She also explained how to get from 729 to zero in three moves.

"I was working with Jenny and I tried her way with eights," said Katie. "I did eight times eight times eight and got 512, then I got to zero in three turns!"

"Sixes work too!" Carl announced. He'd been experimenting on his calculator while Katie was explaining her discovery. "You multiply six times six times six and then you get 216 to start with."

"Would fives work?" I asked. Everyone began multiplying mentally to check this out. They were on a roll.

"That would work, 'cause the answer is 125 and it's still a three-digit number," said Brennan. Brennan was usually disengaged and uninterested in numbers. He struggled with math, but now he was right there with us.

"What about fours?" I asked. "Will four times four times four get us a three-digit number?"

After a few seconds, several students chorused, "No!"

"Why is that?" I asked. I knew that many students in the class knew why, but there are always some who are on the periphery of the conversation, not quite following or understanding. I wanted to give those students a chance to listen to an explanation. I called on Carl.

"Because four times four is 16 and 16 times four is 64," said Carl. "And 64 is not a three-digit number, so we can't start with it."

"Does anyone else have a discovery they'd like to share?"

"This game helps me learn to divide at the right time," said Kerry. "Like when the number is 111, I would know to divide it by an odd number, because 111 is an odd number. If I would divide 111 by two, then it wouldn't come out evenly, because two is an even number. So I think that if the number you're working with is even, then divide it with an even number and if it is odd, then divide it with an odd number." (Kerry's written work is shown in figure 3.5.)

"We're almost out of time, but I think Kerry's conjecture deserves some thought," I told the class. "Kerry, can I write down on the board what you just said so that we can think about it?" I made a point of getting Kerry's permission before opening her conjecture up to scrutiny. Sharing mathematical ideas is risky. I think it's important to maintain an atmosphere of respect during class discussions so that children feel safe expressing their ideas.

On the chalkboard, I wrote: *In this game, divide an odd number by an odd number and an even number by an even number.* "Is this what you mean?" I asked Kerry, pointing to the words. She nodded yes. "Talk about Kerry's statement with someone in your group," I told them. After several minutes, I asked for everyone's attention and called on Michael.

"I think that Kerry's partly right," said Michael. "I think that you can't divide an even number into an odd number evenly and an odd number into an even number evenly. But just because you start with an odd number and divide it by an odd number doesn't mean there'll be no remainder. Like nine divided by five doesn't work."

"Or seven divided by three," added Katie.

"I think you have to think about

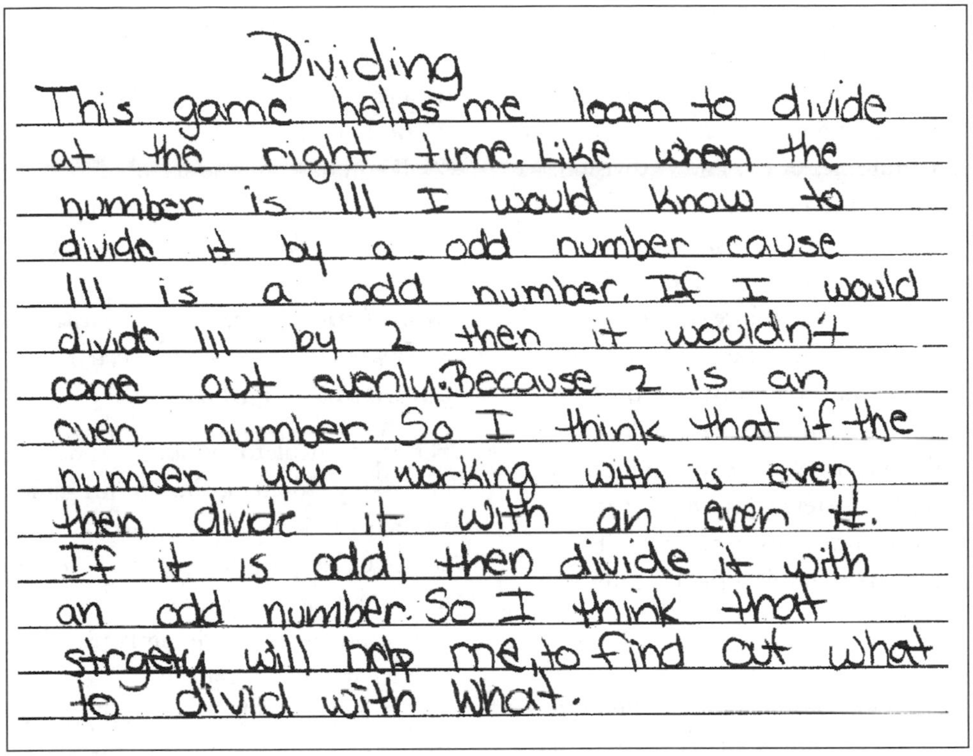

> ## Dividing
>
> This game helps me learn to divide at the right time. Like when the number is 111 I would know to divide it by a odd number cause 111 is a odd number. If I would divide 111 by 2 then it wouldn't come out evenly. Because 2 is an even number. So I think that if the number your working with is even then divide it with an even #. If it is odd, then divide it with an odd number. So I think that stragety will help me, to find out what to divid with What.

FIGURE 3.5

Kerry's faulty conjecture prompted a rich class discussion.

the multiples of a number when you're dividing," said Hannah.

"Kerry's conjecture made us think more about numbers, especially how they're used in division," I said, bringing our class discussion to a close.

RUSTY ANSWERS YOUR QUESTIONS

How does this activity help students develop their number sense?

Facility with computing is an important characteristic of number sense. Get to Zero gives students practice with all the operations, especially division. And using calculators allows them to take risks and try new ways of thinking.

This activity gives students opportunities to think about operations and what happens to quantities when they're added, subtracted, multiplied, and divided. During the activity, for example, Carl revealed his knowledge about division in relation to the other operations when he commented that "you should start with division because it gets you a smaller number." When Anne recommended subtracting till your number ends in zero so that you can divide it by five evenly, she was drawing upon her understanding of the multiples of five and of division. She was using her number sense to think about a strategy.

Get to Zero also gives students the chance to explore the characteristics of numbers: odd and even, factors, multiples, prime and composite. In addition, students are able to learn about decimal numbers, look for patterns, and make conjectures and test hypotheses, all of which help develop their number sense.

How can Get to Zero be modified so that it's more easily accessible?

One way to make this activity more accessible is to start with numbers between 50 and 100 instead of any three-digit number and to use the digits one through five instead of one through nine. Working with smaller numbers is less daunting for students and is therefore a more comfortable place to start.

A colleague of mine taught Get to Zero to her class using only the numbers 50 through 100 and the digits one through five. Then she asked her students to describe strategies they thought were helpful in getting to zero. Here are the strategies they came up with:

1. Choose even numbers.
2. Try to divide by the biggest number you can.
3. If you can't divide, then add or subtract to get to a number that ends in five or zero.
4. Never divide when you have an odd number.
5. If you have an odd number, subtract one, three, or five to get an even number.

Would students need a calculator at home if Get to Zero were a homework assignment?

Having a calculator at home is not necessarily a prerequisite. In this game a calculator is used only to verify computations and to keep track of the numbers as students make their way to zero. Students could certainly play Get to Zero without a calculator.

Although students primarily solve the problems in Get to Zero mentally, they benefit from learning how to use a variety of tools to solve math problems or explore mathematical ideas. A calculator is an important tool that should be available to students in math class.

How would you help students become aware of the divisibility rules?

While some students discover rules for divisibility on their own, it helps to make them explicit so that all students have access to them. Still, students will need a good deal of experience to become comfortable with the divisibility rules. Encourage them to look for patterns. Some are easy to recognize, such as counting by fives and noticing that all the multiples end in zero or five, or learning that all even numbers are multiples of two. But the discovery that if the sum of the digits in a number is a multiple of three (for example, 123, or 1 + 2 + 3 = 6), then the number is a multiple of three is not as obvious.

The benefit of a game like Get to Zero is that it provides a reason for students to think about divisibility, another valuable way to understand relationships among numbers.

The Basics and More

*T*raditionally, the "basics" were single-digit number facts and computation, and they are still basic components of mathematics. But how can we help our students become competent with the basics in a way that simultaneously develops their number sense? To do that, math instruction in classrooms needs to accommodate and encourage a variety of computational techniques.

In the old days, arithmetic procedures were taught by modeling and explaining each step of an algorithm: "Start on the right, put down the one, carry the ten. . . ." Rules were memorized, procedures were standardized. There was little room for improvisation and little concern for understanding.

However, it's important for students to realize that mathematical rules and procedures were discovered by mathematicians who recognized certain inherent properties of numbers. Students in math class need to behave like mathematicians and discover the wonders of numbers for themselves. Class discussions about different ways to think about computation are extremely valuable ways to foster this discovery.

Proficiency with the components of computation remains essential. But students also need latitude in their thinking about numbers if they are to develop number sense. Repetitive exercises with isolated numbers do not suffice. Students need to be able to make sense of what they are doing. When students share their own computational strategies, everyone in the class benefits from hearing a variety of approaches. The act of listening to and making sense of someone else's approach to numbers and computation forces the listeners to expand their horizons. As students hear about and understand more ways to think about numbers, they augment their own mathematical abilities. They become more flexible thinkers who have more than one way to deal with a novel problem when it arises. They are able to see the inherent usefulness of mathematics. They remain curious and enthusiastic learners.

While all the activities presented in this book provide teachers with new ways to think about the basics of math, the three in this section concentrate heavily on number calculations and combinations. They offer ways to help students learn the basics and at the same time support the development of number sense.

4 *One Time Only*

Understanding Factors, Multiples and Prime Numbers

Overview

Upper elementary students benefit from activities that help reinforce their understanding of factors, multiples, and prime numbers. In this two-person game, students take turns identifying factors of successive numbers, continuing until one of them can no longer contribute a new number.

Directions for Playing the Game

1. Player 1 writes down a number greater than one and less than 100.

2. Player 2 writes down a factor of the first number underneath it.

3. Player 1 writes down a factor of this new number.

4. Each player, taking turns, writes down a factor of the preceding number.

5. If a player writes down a prime number (i.e., it is not divisible without a remainder by any other integers except one and itself), the next player adds seven to it and writes down the resulting sum as his or her turn.

6. The player who can no longer contribute a new number loses the game.

Additional Rules

1. Once a number has been written down, it can't be used again.

2. The number one can't be used at all.

IN THE CLASSROOM WITH CAREN

Introducing the Activity

"Today I have a game for you," I announced to the sixth graders in Lyndsey Lovelace and Shea Carrillo's class. "It's called One Time Only. To play the game you need a partner. One of the partners begins by picking a number greater than one and less than 100. So you can see how it works, the whole class will be my partner for this first game. There are just a few rules, and I'll explain them while we play."

I wrote *36* on the overhead.

"Now it's your turn," I said. "You need to think of a factor of 36. Can anyone tell me a number that goes evenly into 36? Another way to think about it is by skip counting. Which numbers can you skip count by and get to 36?"

By introducing several ways to think about factors, I hoped to explain the game more quickly. If I'd just asked for a factor of 36, students who weren't sure what a factor was or who weren't sure about the difference between a factor and a multiple might not have been able to participate. As the students used the terminology in the context of the game, they'd become more comfortable with it.

"So, what do you think?" I asked. "Can anyone tell me a factor of 36?"

"How about six?" offered Fred.

"Is six a factor of 36?" I asked the class.

Several students nodded or vocalized their assent. I pushed for more of a commitment. "Who can explain why they think six is a factor of 36?" I asked.

Jessie raised her hand. "Because six times six is 36," she explained.

"Also," added José, "if you count by sixes you'll say 36. Like 6, 12, 18, 24, 30 36."

"All right," I said, "I'm convinced that six is a factor of 36." I wrote *6* under *36* on a projected transparency. "Now I need to find a factor of six to add to the chain of numbers we're making here. I think I'll say two." I wrote *2* under the *6*. "Okay, now it's your turn to think of a factor of two," I said.

"Two," said Derek. "Two times one is two."

"Well, yes," I responded, "two is a factor of itself, but one rule is that you can't use the same number twice. That's why the game is called One Time Only. If a number is already written down you can't use it again. Can anyone think of a factor of two that's not already up here?" I asked, pointing to the overhead.

"One," said Ali.

"Well, that brings up another rule in One Time Only. You can't use one. You're correct, Ali, that one is a factor of two. But in this game you're not allowed to use one. So you can't use a number that's already up there and you can't use one. Those are the two main rules of this game. Can you think of any other factors of two?"

"How about four?" asked Chrissy.

"How do you know four is a factor of two?" I inquired.

"Because two times two equals

four," Chrissy explained. Chrissy had confused factors and multiples. I was glad she had made the multiplication connection, but I needed to prompt her a bit to get her back on track.

"I know that two is a factor of four, because I can count to four by twos," I said to her. "But it doesn't work the other way around. Four isn't a factor of two, because you can't count to two by fours."

"Oh, yeah," Chrissy replied.

"Does anyone know what we call four in this situation?" I asked the class.

"A multiple!" exclaimed Neal. "If you can times a number to get the number it's a multiple. Like 36 is a multiple of six because six times six is 36."

"All right," I continued, "so are there any factors of two besides two and one?"

"Can we use fractions?" asked Howard.

"Sorry," I told him, "but factors need to be whole numbers, like the regular numbers you use when you're counting. So are there any other factors of two?" I kept posing the problem to get students really to think about two and its relationship to other numbers. This sort of thinking builds number sense. Also, I wanted the students to convince themselves that two only had two factors. "Take a minute and talk at your tables," I suggested. "See if you

can think of any other factors of two."

I let the students talk briefly and then I called them back to attention. "Did any tables find any other factors of two?" I asked. The class consensus was no. "So, do you think there are any other factors of two?" I prodded, checking to see if the students were really convinced.

"Not if we can't use fractions," Ana qualified.

"Well," I told the class, "you're right. There are only two factors of two, two and one. Does anyone know what you call a number that only has itself and one as factors?"

"Prime?" Greg ventured in a barely audible tone.

"Prime!" several students announced with authority after hearing Greg.

"Yes, those are prime numbers." I wrote *prime* next to *2* on the overhead. "A number that only has itself and one for factors is called a prime number. In One Time Only when you hit a prime number you add seven to it.[1] So what's two plus seven?"

"Nine," several students responded.

I wrote *9* on the overhead under the *2*.

"Okay, now it's my turn, and I need to think of a factor of nine. I'll say three," I said, as I added *3* to the list on the overhead. "Now you need to find a factor of three."

---

[1]Adding seven to the prime numbers extends the game, which would otherwise end when the first prime number occurred. It might be interesting to add a number other than seven to the primes and see how that affects the outcome.

"It's prime," announced Natalie with authority.

"Are you sure about that?" I asked the rest of the class.

"Yes, it is," agreed Jasper, "because three times one is three and that's it."

"If it's prime, what happens?" I asked.

"Add seven," José reminded us. "So it's ten."

I wrote *prime* next to the *3* and put a *10* below it.

"How many times can you use plus seven?" Jessie asked.

"There's no limit," I explained. "Anytime you're playing and a prime number comes up, you just add seven to it. It's my turn again and I need to put a factor of ten that's not already listed. I'll say five."

"Oh no," exclaimed Alejandro, "another prime number for us."

I raised my eyebrows in feigned surprise as I looked at the numbers on the overhead. "Wow, it *is* a prime number." I agreed. "You keep getting prime numbers on your turn. I wonder if that always happens in this game. Maybe there's some kind of pattern." While I knew that this particular pattern didn't always happen, I took the opportunity to spark a little curiosity. I hoped that in subsequent games students would pay more attention to the occurrence of patterns in general as they played. Looking for patterns is a powerful way to build number sense, particularly when students have opportunities to think about the patterns and their relationships to numbers and operations. I referred to the string of numbers on the overhead, which now looked like this:

36

6

2 prime

9

3 prime

10

5 prime

"Okay," I said to the class, "it's your turn and since five is prime, what do you need to do?"

"Add seven," Jasper replied.

"Right," I agreed, "so now it's 12." I wrote *12* on the overhead. "Hmm," I said, "I need to find a factor of 12 that's not already up here." I paused for a few seconds to give students a chance to review the numbers and think about factors of 12. I also wanted the students to see that math involves taking time to think.

"I know," I brightened, "I'll say four." I wrote *4* on the overhead beneath the *12.* "Now you need to find a factor of four that's not already up here. Talk at your tables for a minute or two and see what you can come up with."

"We're stuck," Ali soon announced.

"What do you mean?" I asked.

"Well," Fred explained, "we're not allowed to use one. Four and two are used already. There are no other factors, so we can't go."

"Does everyone agree with Fred and Ali?" I asked, looking around.

The nods and yeahs were unanimous.

"Then I guess the game is over," I said. "This time I won, because I was the last player to add a number to the list. You want to get your partner stuck so she or he is unable to add a number to the string. But winning isn't really the important part of this game. You're going to play a bunch of times, and sometimes you'll win and sometimes you'll lose. The important part of the game is the mathematical thinking that you do."

I played one more game with the whole class. This second game went more quickly, because I didn't need to stop to explain the rules and vocabulary. After two games, I was satisfied that the students understood the rules and knew how to determine a winner. The factor concept had been reinforced, the term *multiple* had been introduced in context, and the students knew how to identify prime numbers.

"Raise your hand if you understand One Time Only and you're ready to play with your partner," I instructed the class. The students were ready. "I want you to know the plan for the rest of this math class," I told them. "You definitely need to have some more time to play One Time Only so you get familiar with it. Before the end of class we're going to get back together and have a discussion about your experiences playing the game. I'm interested in hearing about any strategies you used to help you win the game. We'll also talk about any tricky numbers that came up while you were playing."

"What do you mean?" asked Katrine.

"By tricky numbers I mean numbers that aren't so easy to find factors for," I elaborated. "Some numbers are pretty easy because they come up a lot on the multiplication table. But there are other numbers between 1 and 100 that you don't use very much when you're doing basic multiplication facts, 47 for example. It will be interesting to hear which numbers you ran into that were kind of tricky and how you found factors for them."

Observing the Students

As the students began to play, I visited the tables. Most of the children had paired up and begun playing without much prompting. There were a few discussions about who got to go first and who had to keep score. These issues were easily resolved by flipping a coin or playing rock/paper/scissors. Most of the students organized their recording sheets the way I had. Some, like Juan and Vivian, also kept track of how many games each player won.

The two whole-class games we played each had three prime numbers in them, but Katrine and Shante excitedly reported they had just finished a game in which four prime numbers appeared. I announced this milestone to the class at large. Conversations erupted throughout the classroom about prime numbers and how many times they had been encountered in different games.

Ana and Ronald were stuck on 97. Ana got a calculator from the shelf. "Divide it by something," Ronald told her.

Ana punched in 97 divided by three and got 32.33. "What does that mean?" she asked Ronald.

"It's not right—you can't divide it by three. There's a decimal. That means it didn't divide evenly." Ronald explained. "Try seven."

Ana found that 97 divided by seven was 18.85. "Nope," she told Ronald. The pair continued to guess and check by dividing 97 by six and four. "I think it's prime," was Ana's appraisal.

"It is," agreed Ronald.

"Are you sure?" I asked. "What about dividing 97 by five? You didn't try that."

"Well," Ana explained, "five will definitely have a decimal, because 97 doesn't end with zero or five. When you count by fives the numbers always end with zero or five."

Impromptu discussions like this are an excellent opportunity to help students build their number sense. Ronald and Ana were thinking about numbers, their relationships and patterns, and the implications of a decimal. As I continued to circulate, I tried to help the children focus on the numbers.

Fred and José were eager to start with a number greater than 100. I asked them to stick with numbers less than 100 for the moment, but I agreed that using larger numbers would be an interesting investigation for the future.

A Class Discussion

I called the class back together when there were about fifteen minutes left in the period. "I have some questions to ask you about the game, but before I start, do any of you have a question or comment?" I began.

Enrique had an interesting scenario: "What if you start the game with 97?" (He had been sitting near Ana and Ronald.) "That's the highest prime number, but when you add seven to it you go over 100, and you're only supposed to use numbers less than 100."

"Wow," I replied, "I hadn't thought about that. I'd say it's okay to use 97, because it's less than 100. You might need to write down a number larger than 100 for one turn, but I don't think it will last." Then I decided to open the door for further investigation. "I wonder if there are any other high prime numbers that could put you over 100 when you add seven?" I hoped that in future games some students might choose to pursue this question.

"Let's talk about your strategies," I suggested. "For example, when Elliot was playing, he told me he thought it was a good idea to start with an odd number. This was his strategy to help him win the game. Did anyone have any other strategies that seemed useful?"

Natalie's hand shot up. "I concentrated on six."

"What do you mean?" I asked.

"Well," she explained, "I tried to end with the number six. But first I tried to get rid of all the factors of six, like three and two, so that way when I wrote down six, I knew my partner couldn't do anything. Also, if you get rid of the factors of six, you're also getting rid of the factors of nine and four."

"It worked," said Natalie's partner, Juanita.

"What other strategies did you use?" I asked the class.

"Try to end with an even number," advised Jessie.

"Start with an odd number," Katrine added.

As the students shared their strategies, I recorded each one on a projected transparency. Alejandro had an idea to add to the list.

"My strategy was to get rid of three and then give my partner nine."

Natalie had more to say. "This isn't a winning strategy," she qualified as she began, "it's a winning pattern. In our games we had this pattern, two, nine, three, ten, five, twelve, six."

"Hey," interjected José, "we had the same pattern!"

"We had almost the same pattern," Shante piped in. "But ours is two, nine, three, ten, five, twelve, four."

"This is very interesting," I confirmed. "As you play more I wonder if you'll find more patterns. I'm also wondering if seeing these patterns can help you predict who's going to win." These were not questions that could be answered during the current whole-class discussion, but I was confident they would be explored more intently over time. The students needed more experience playing the game and thinking about the implications of these patterns—why they emerged, and how they might be manipulated. Often a whole-class discussion is not a neat and tidy wrap-up but rather an occasion to raise questions that lead into deeper mathematical territory.

"There's one other thing I want to ask about," I continued. "Did anyone encounter a tricky number? What were some of the numbers that were hard to find factors for?" I gathered a bunch of responses quickly and wrote all the numbers on the chalkboard under the heading "Tricky Numbers." The list included 75, 26, 47, 89, 11, 68, 17, 44, 59, 99, and 62.

A Homework Assignment

I had tried to emphasize thinking throughout the activity. However, while I had focused on certain questions during the session, I couldn't be sure how much the students were really thinking about the ideas I posed. With thirty-two students in a class, it's difficult to get to everyone. Also, the whole-class discussion we had after the students played allowed some but not all students to express their ideas. Having each student write would give me a window into their thinking.

"I am really interested in knowing more about your thinking," I told the class. "Therefore, I have a homework assignment for you. There are just two questions for you to answer, but you need to try to explain your answers fully so I'll understand how you thought about these questions. The first question asks you to think about the number 68 and different ways you can find the factors of 68. The other job is for you to teach One Time Only to someone at home and write about the strategies you used to try to win."

I chose the number 68 because I

knew it had factors but it wasn't a number that occurs in the context of typical multiplication tables. The students would need to think about quantities and their relationships rather than just spit back some memorized numbers.

The students had many methods for finding factors. Several of the students outlined specific systematic approaches to the task. Others described a trial-and-error process. Rolanda's response to the first question showed she was able to take 68 apart in several helpful ways:

> *1. If it is an even number then you would be able to split it in half.*
> *2. You could times 4 by 10 and get 40. Then 4 times 5 is 20, so that's 60 and then we all already know that 2 fours is 8, so that's 68.*
> *3. Another easy way is to just divide 68 by another number and if you get a whole number then you have a factor. 2, 4, 34, 17, 68. I know that all these are the factors of 68 because I used my methods on all of the numbers smaller than 34 because any number larger than 34 is not a factor. They are not factors because any number larger than 34 would go over 68 if you times it by 2.*

The descriptions of strategies were enlightening as well. I was able to see the different ways students thought about the game and the different ways they expressed themselves in writing. Shannon gave a detailed plan with an explanation for each step: *If you go first pick a prime number. Then the opponent will have to add seven. It will become a*

even number. Your turn, divide the number by half of the number. You will get 2 on the board. The number is prime again. The opponent will now have to add 7. You will get 9 (7 + 2 = 9). Your turn again. Divide 9 by 3. You will get 3. Another prime number. Again the opponent will have to add 7. You get 10 (3 + 7 = 10). Divide it by 2 and you get 5. Once again a prime number. The opponent adds 7 (5 + 7 = 12). You get 12. Now divide 12 by 2 and you get 6. For once it is not a prime number for the opponent. The factors for this number that are allowed are 2 and 3. But wait a minute. We already used 2, and 3. So the person who started this game won.

A few of the students' writing was vague. It was difficult to know whether their thinking was unclear or whether it was the writing that was difficult. I'd need to get back to these students individually.

CAREN ANSWERS YOUR QUESTIONS

What is the purpose of this activity?

One Time Only is a great opportunity for students to develop their number sense. The game context engages them, and the discussions they have with their partner help them think about numbers. Their experiences during the game become the basis for some substantial whole-class discussions about important topics. Asking them to write about the game gives them an opportunity to clarify their thinking. As the students continue to play One

Time Only, they build on their previous experiences and further develop their number sense.

Would you play this game with third graders?

I wouldn't introduce this game to third graders at the beginning of the year. It's important that they have a good foundation in multiplication first. If the students are unfamiliar with the concept of multiplication and the relationship of factors to products, then One Time Only could be frustrating or turn into a guessing game.

However, once third graders have a solid grasp of multiplication, One Time Only is an excellent way for them to reinforce the basic facts while exploring ways to think about factors of different numbers. With third graders I'd spend extra time talking about ways to find factors before I sent them off to play on their own. That way they'd have some tools available if they got stuck.

What do students get from this game if they already know their multiplication facts?

In addition to practicing multiplication facts, students who play One Time Only are exploring the number system. As students play the game, they begin to develop strategies. In order to devise a winning strategy students must consider the relationships of numbers. For example,

Brittany noticed that the factors of six are also factors of four and nine. Seeing these connections between numbers helps build number sense.

Also, as students examine their records of the games they've played, patterns emerge. These patterns are another opportunity to develop number sense. Teachers can ask their students to think about why certain patterns recur, what causes these numbers to arise in a specific order, and how the patterns can help predict the outcome of a game. The game provides many occasions for writing, as well.

Amanda and Ronald used a calculator. Is this appropriate?

Amanda and Ronald were trying to find factors of 97. When their knowledge of basic multiplication facts failed them, they used a calculator. I felt fine about it. A calculator is a tool to be used in service of a problem. Amanda and Ronald had a problem and knew that dividing 97 by different numbers would tell them something about its factors. When Amanda and Ronald couldn't think of any factors for 97, I could have jumped in and told them that 97 was prime. Instead, I gave them the freedom to delve further. It turned out to be a double learning opportunity. In addition to convincing themselves that 97 was prime, they also confronted decimals and had to make sense of their meaning.

5 *Tell Me All You Can*

Overview

Computing mentally, making estimates, and exploring relationships among numbers all help students develop number sense. In this activity, students tell all they can about the answers to a series of arithmetic problems. While they may know the exact answer to a problem, the activity requires them to think about ways to describe the answer using concepts such as close to, between, greater than, and less than.

Teaching Directions

1. Write an arithmetic problem on the chalkboard using a horizontal format (for example: 30×11).

2. After giving students time to think about the problem, ask them what they can say about the answer without actually revealing the answer (regarding 30×11, for example: "I think the answer will be more than 300 because 30 times ten is 300").

3. After eliciting as many responses as possible, repeat steps 1 and 2 with another arithmetic problem.

IN THE CLASSROOM WITH RUSTY

Introducing the Activity to Fifth Graders

I began the activity in Sally Haggerty's fifth-grade classroom by writing *12 × 7* horizontally on the chalkboard, since the vertical format often triggers the algorithm of starting from the right and "carrying." I wanted students to look at the numbers as a whole and to think about the largest parts of the numbers first.

"Without figuring the exact answer, what are some things you know about the answer?" I asked the class. I waited while the students thought about my question, then I called on Damarie.

"I think the answer is going to be less than 120, because 12 times ten is 120," she said.

"I think the answer is going to be greater than 60 because I know that 12 times five is 60," said Jimmy.

Jay interjected, "You mean we don't have to figure the exact answer?"

"That's right," I replied. "I want you to look at the problem and think about the numbers, then tell me something about the answer."

"What if we can find out the answer in our head right away?" Carole asked.

"That's okay," I said. "If you know the answer, try to talk about it without saying the answer. It's important to think about a problem and its answer in lots of different ways. It helps our math thinking if we make estimates

about the answer to a problem, because it gives us a sense of how big or how small the exact answer is going to be, and it also helps us focus on what the numbers mean. Does anyone have something else to say about the answer to 12 times seven?"

"I think it's going to be more than 12 times six, because that's six 12s and 12 times seven is seven 12s," said Miriam.

At this point, I wrote the following prompts on the chalkboard and told the students that they could use them to talk about the answers to the problems I was about to give them:

- The answer is going to be around/about _____ because _____.
- The answer is going to be close to _____ because _____.
- The answer is going to be between _____ and _____ because _____.
- The answer is going to be greater than _____ because _____.
- The answer is going to be less than _____ because _____.

Then I wrote another problem on the chalkboard: *30 × 11*. "What can you say about the answer?" I asked the class. Soon, several hands popped up. I waited a few more seconds, and more hands raised. I called on Kathy.

"I think it will be more than 300, 'cause 30 times ten is 300," she said. Students who use their number sense will often look at a problem holistically before confronting details. Instead of focusing on individual digits, Kathy first thought about 30, then she multiplied 30 by ten, which is close to but less than 11, yielding a pretty good approximation of the answer.

"What else can you say about the answer to 30 times 11?" I continued.

"It's going to be more than 320," said Tom.

"Why do you think that?" I asked.

"I don't know," he replied.

"I want you to try to give a reason for your estimates," I told the class. "That way, your classmates will benefit from listening to your thinking, and your teacher and I will learn more about how you reason with numbers. What else can you say about 30 times 11?"

"It's going to be less than 400, because I know that 30 times ten is 300 and there's only one more 30, which is less than 100," Chrissy reasoned.

"Other ideas?" I asked. No one raised a hand. My plan was to pose a variety of problems, some easy, some more difficult, because I wanted everyone to have access to the conversation. I wrote another problem on the chalkboard: 25×7. As soon as I did, lots of hands waved in the air.

"It's going to be greater than 100, because 25 times four is 100," said Carole.

"I think it'll be more than 150, because six quarters are \$1.50," Miguel added.

"It will be less than 200, because eight times 25 is 200," said José. "I know that because four 25s are 100, and double that and it's 200."

More hands wiggled in the air. Although I could have used any problem for this activity, 25×7

seemed to invite a great deal of participation, perhaps because it involved a familiar number like 25.

"It's going to be more than 170, because 25 times four is 100, and if you add another two 25s it's 150, and you still have to add another 25," Courtney explained.

The students didn't seem to mind that we never said what the answers to the problems were. Although finding exact answers is important in math class, it isn't the point of this activity. I wanted students to begin to feel comfortable taking risks and making estimates based on mathematical reasoning. Being able to discuss a problem without having to come up with an exact answer often reduces students' anxiety about math. (This is true for adults as well.)

When everyone who wished to had contributed, I wrote the next equation on the chalkboard: 75×12. This problem drew some oohs and ahs. It was more difficult than the previous problems I'd posed. When no one raised a hand after a while, I asked a question that I hoped would stimulate their thinking: "Will the answer be more or less than 100?" This seemed obvious, but I wanted to start at a safe place so students would feel comfortable participating.

"It's going to be a lot bigger than 100!" exclaimed Chrissy. "Seventy-five times two is more than 100, and the problem is 75 times 12!"

"I want you to talk with someone next to you about what you think about the answer to 75 times 12," I told them. In a moment, I called the students back to attention.

"I think it's going to be a lot bigger than 150, because 75 times two is 150, and you have to go ten times bigger than that," Miguel reasoned.

"It'll be bigger than 750, 'cause 75 times ten is 750, and it's 75 times 12, not 75 times ten," added Courtney.

"It's easy," said Dave. "You just do what Courtney said, 75 times ten, and you get 750, then you do two more 75s and add that to 750. It'll be between 800 and 900."

"It'll be more than 825, because 75 times ten is 750, and 75 times 11 is 750 plus 75, which is 825," explained Carolee.

When we finished discussing 75 × 12, I posed a problem that included fractions, even though I knew Sally hadn't yet begun a unit on fractions this year. I wasn't sure what kinds of responses I'd get from students, but listening to their responses would let Sally and me assess what students knew about fractions. I wrote $\frac{1}{2} + \frac{1}{3}$ on the chalkboard. After a brief amount of think time, I called on Miguel.

"I think it's going to be around one fourth because . . ." Miguel hesitated, then continued. "Because one half plus one third is . . . I can't explain it, but I know that it's going to be about one fourth."

I didn't push Miguel to try to explain at this point. I wanted to give him a chance to listen to other ideas, so I called on Courtney.

"It's going to be bigger than three fourths, because a half is two fourths, and a third is bigger than a fourth," Courtney explained. "And two fourths plus one fourth is three fourths."

"How do you know that one third is bigger than one fourth?" I asked.

"Because if you had one pizza and it had three equal parts, each piece is bigger than if you had a pizza with four equal parts," said Courtney. "If there were four pieces of pizza, then one person would get a smaller piece than if the pizza was cut in thirds." Courtney had a picture of fractions as portions of a pizza that helped her reason through the problem using her number sense. In contrast, a student for whom fractions have no meaning often sees two digits separated by a horizontal bar and is likely to make the classic mistake of adding the numerator and denominator: $\frac{1}{2} + \frac{1}{3} = \frac{2}{5}$.

"Would someone like to come up and draw a picture of the two pizzas that Courtney is talking about?" I asked the class. It was hard to choose among so many enthusiastic hand wavers, so I quickly called on Miguel. I wanted to give him another opportunity to be involved. He walked to the front of the room, drew two pizzas the same size, and divided them: one into three equal parts, the other into four equal parts. "Does this help support Courtney's thinking that one third is bigger than one fourth?" I asked.

All heads except Chrissy's nodded. "I agree, except what if one of the pizzas was a large and the other one was a medium?" Chrissy asked. "If the large was cut into fourths and the medium was cut into thirds, I think one fourth could be bigger than one third."

"So it depends on whether the

wholes are the same size," I clarified. "If the two pizzas are the same size, is Courtney correct in saying that one third is larger than one fourth?"

"Uh-huh," Chrissy replied.

"What else can you say about the answer?" I asked the class. This time, no one raised a hand. "Do you think the answer will be less than or greater than one whole?" I prompted. "Talk with someone next to you and tell her or him what you think and why, then listen to that person's explanation." In a moment, I called them back to attention.

"I think the answer's going to be less than one, because one half plus one half is a whole, and one half is bigger than one third," said Dave. "So one half plus one third would have to be smaller than one."

"I agree with Dave," said Damarie.

"Does anyone have a different idea?" I probed.

"I think the answer will be between three fourths and one whole, because if it was one half plus one fourth it would be three fourths," explained Miriam. "But since one third is bigger than one fourth, the answer's going to be bigger than three fourths but less than one because of what Dave said."

This conversation yielded the kind of reasoning that's beneficial to students when taking standardized tests. On multiple-choice test items, students usually have three or four answers from which to choose. Generally, a few of those answers are unreasonable. When students use their number sense to reason through a problem and make an estimate, they can often eliminate unreasonable answers.

I continued the activity, posing another fraction problem: $^7/_8 + ^8/_9$. Before eliciting responses from the students, I asked them to talk with one another about the problem first.

Observing the Students

As I walked around the room, listening to their conversations, I noticed that some students had no idea what to say about the answer, while others were immediately engaged. Alberto, who was sitting next to Joseph, was having difficulty thinking about the fractions and what they meant.

"What can you say about the answer?" I asked Alberto.

"I don't know," he answered, giggling nervously.

"Let's take a look at one of the fractions," I suggested. "Is seven eighths closer to zero, one half, or a whole?" My question was intended to provide Alberto with a way of thinking about the fractions.

"A half?" Alberto responded, unsure and looking confused. His answer sounded like a guess.

Joseph jumped in. "I think it's close to a whole," he said.

"Why's that?" I asked.

"Because it's like if you had a pizza with eight pieces and you ate seven out of eight, it's almost the whole thing," Joseph explained. Pizzas seemed to be a popular model for thinking about fractions.

I turned to Alberto, who was still wearing a confused look. "Alberto, draw a pizza with eight slices and make each slice the same size, okay?" I said. He nodded, and drew the pizza. "Now shade in seven pieces, like you're eating those seven pieces of pizza," I directed. After Alberto had shaded in the pieces, I asked him if the pieces he'd shaded were closer to one half of the pizza or closer to the whole pizza. His face lit up. I could see that he was beginning to make sense of the problem.

As I made my way around the room, I thought about students, like Alberto, who needed support in order to think about the problem. To develop an understanding about fractions, these students would need to have experience with many different kinds of concrete models—not only pizzas! Understanding what fractions are is important, especially if students are asked to add, subtract, multiply, or divide them.

Continuing the Activity

After a few minutes, I called the class back together and asked what they could say about the answer.

"Well, it's going to be bigger than a whole because seven eighths is bigger than a half," said Tamim. "Four eighths is the same thing as a half, and seven eighths is almost twice as big. Then you've got the other eight ninths to add to that."

"I rounded seven eighths off to eight eighths, which is the same as one whole," Marcellus offered. "Then I rounded eight ninths to nine ninths, which is another whole. So that's almost two wholes right there."

"Other ideas?" I asked.

"The answer's going to be a mixed number," Brittany stated with confidence. "Like Marcellus said, the answer's going to be about two. I think a little less than two, because each fraction is a little less than one. So the answer's going to be one whole and a fraction."

I liked this problem because it required students to think about the quantities involved rather than focus on the standard algorithm used to add fractions with unlike denominators. Finding an approximate answer is an important exercise that helps students develop their number sense.

The final problem I posed to Sally's fifth graders involved division: *450 ÷ 75*. Again, I had them talk with a partner about the answer before we discussed our ideas as a class.

After about a minute or so, I asked the students what they could say about the answer. The room was quiet, with no hands raised. To stimulate the students' thinking, I asked a question I'd thought about beforehand. Preparation like this is important before teaching an activity like Tell Me All You Can.

"Thumbs up if you think the answer will be more than ten and thumbs down if you think the answer will be less than ten," I instructed. Most thumbs were pointing down. "Can you explain your reasoning?"

"Because 75 times ten is 750, and that's too big," said Brittany.

"Seventy-five times two is 150, then I doubled that, so 75 times four is 300, then 75 times eight is double 300, which is 600, and that's too big," explained Andy. "So if 75 times eight is bigger than 450, then the answer has to be less than ten."

"Will the answer be more or less than five?" I asked.

"It's gonna be between five and ten," Franco said. " We know it's less than ten, and it's gonna be more than five, because if 75 times ten is 750, then half of that is 75 times five, and that's 375," he reasoned.

"I think it's closer to six or seven, because of what Franco just said," added Ahmad.

Afterward, Sally commented that she could easily use Tell Me All You Can as a math class opener. We both agreed that with practice her students would get better at finding different ways to approximate answers to arithmetic problems.

Introducing the Activity to Third Graders

Just as I'd done in Sally's classroom, I wrote problems on the chalkboard horizontally for Maryann Wickett's third graders to think about. The first one was: *$10.00 – $1.99.* "What can you say about the answer to this problem?" I asked. The students were huddled close to me on the rug in the front of the classroom.

"The answer's gonna be less than ten dollars, 'cause you take money away from ten dollars," said Tiffany.

"It's gonna be twelve dollars!" Miguel blurted out. His answer triggered several disconcerted looks. It's not uncommon for students to disregard an operation sign as Miguel had done.

Since mistakes are opportunities for learning, I probed his thinking. "How did you figure?"

Miguel stared at the problem on the board, then his face lit up. "Oh!" he exclaimed. "I need to do take-away."

"So it's important to look at the operation sign to see if you have to add, subtract, multiply, or divide," I said to the class. "The signs tell us what to do with the numbers." I quickly moved on to another student, satisfied that this important point had been made.

"It's going to be around eight dollars, because $1.99 is only a penny less than two dollars, and ten minus two is eight," Andy explained.

"That's what I was gonna say," Jessica agreed.

These responses impressed me; the students were using their knowledge about operations and working with friendly numbers. Had they figured the answer to $10.00 – $1.99 using the standard algorithm for subtraction, they'd be doing lots of "borrowing," most likely with little concern for comparing the quantities involved.

"Okay, I have another problem for you to think about," I said. I wrote it on the chalkboard: *45 + 45 + 45.*

"It's gonna be between 100 and 150," said Jesycha. "I guesstimated!"

"What made you think of numbers between 100 and 150?" I asked.

"Because 45 plus 45 is 90, and there's another 45, so the answer's gonna be somewhere in between 100 and 150," she explained.

"I'm thinking of it like 45 times three, because 45 times three is the same as 45 plus 45 plus 45," said Manuel.

"I think you should turn each 45 into a 50, because it's easier," added Tammy. "Fifty plus 50 plus 50 is 150, so I think the answer's going to be around 150."

"Any other ideas?" I asked.

"The answer's going to end in a 5, 'cause five plus five plus five is 15," said Elba.

When no one else had an idea, I posed my final problem: *49 – 25*.

"The answer's going to be around 25," Elba said. "I changed the 49 into a 50, and I know that 50 minus 25 is like 25 cents."

"It's gonna be under 50, because 49 is close to 50 and you take away 25," added Andy.

"I changed the 49 into 45," Sarah reported. "Then I did 45 minus 25, so the answer's gonna be around 20, because 25 plus ten is 35, plus ten more is 45."

"The answer will be the same as 12 times two," reported Dan, who'd solved the problem in his head and then found another way to express it.

When the activity was over, I commented to Maryann that her students seemed comfortable with it.

"That's because they've had lots of practice thinking about numbers in different ways," she reminded me.

Maryann and I agreed that third graders are just beginning to use computational estimation and that learning to approximate answers to arithmetic problems takes time and experience.

RUSTY ANSWERS YOUR QUESTIONS

What is the purpose of this activity?

Tell Me All You Can can be used in almost any grade level to give students practice with arithmetic while building their number sense. In an activity like this, students have opportunities to think about reasonableness, place value, and number meaning. They also benefit from the chance to acquire new computation and estimation strategies.

Why is an activity like this better than procedural drills?

Children benefit from frequent practice solving arithmetic problems, but the practice they get in this activity asks them to think about the numbers involved and what happens to these numbers when they are added, subtracted, multiplied, and divided. Rather than learning a certain procedure and practicing it over and over, students are encouraged to think about the reasonableness of their estimates and explain their reasoning. This kind of practice builds a student's number sense.

How can I make sure this activity will be effective?

It's important to pose a variety of problems, some easy, some more challenging. This allows more students to have access to the thinking that's required. Students also need time to think about the problems and talk with one another in order to clarify their ideas and get more than one perspective. Students always need to explain their reasoning, so that others can benefit from their thinking. Finally, as the teacher, you need to think about the problems beforehand and develop possible questions that will stimulate students' thinking.

How can I use this activity for assessment purposes?

This activity gave Sally Haggerty an idea of the range of understanding her fifth graders had about fractions. This was valuable to her, since she hadn't yet begun teaching her students about fractions. One thing she learned was that many of her students used pizza as their only model when thinking about fractions. She realized she would need to offer them a variety of models to help them construct their understanding.

Knowing what experience and understanding students bring to a topic in math is important, because when we learn something new, we build on what we already know. Sometimes what we know makes mathematical sense and sometimes it doesn't. An activity like Tell Me All You Can can alert you to students' misunderstandings or lack of experience.

6 *Trail Mix for a Crowd*

Overview

Students benefit from experiences that help them connect abstract ideas about fractions to real-world contexts. In this activity, students are given a recipe for trail mix that serves six people. The measurements include fractions, and the students' task is to convert the recipe so that there is enough trail mix to serve everyone in the class.

Materials Needed

Copies of a recipe for trail mix (one per student).
An overhead transparency of the recipe (optional).
Calculators (one per student or table).

Teaching Directions

1. Distribute a copy of the recipe to each student and, if you like, display a transparency of the recipe on an overhead projector.

2. Review the recipe with the students, clarifying the ingredients and any measurement abbreviations.

3. Have the students determine the number of people in the class.

4. Choose one ingredient for the whole class to convert into the larger amount required for the recipe to serve everyone in the class. Have students work in groups to determine how much of this ingredient would be required.

5. As a class, discuss different approaches.

6. Have students convert the rest of the ingredients and rewrite the recipe so that it serves the number of people in the class.

7. Discuss estimation and accuracy with the students.

Extension

Discuss situations in which accuracy is necessary and situations in which estimation is appropriate or even preferable.

Blackline Master

Trail Mix

Trail mix is a healthy snack food. It got its name from hikers and backpackers who ate it on their journeys.

You will need:

$1/2$ cup raisins
$3/4$ cup peanuts
$2/3$ cup granola
$1/2$ cup dried fruit
2 tablespoons sunflower seeds
$1/4$ cup M&Ms

Combine ingredients in bowl. Mix well. Scoop into baggies for a snack on the go.

Serves 6

IN THE CLASSROOM WITH CAREN

Introducing the Activity

I wanted to present Kathleen Gallagher's thirty-two fifth graders with an opportunity to grapple with fractions in a meaningful context. My goal was to give them a problem in which fractions were integral. I wanted the task to be understandable, but I didn't want the computational approach(es) to be obvious. What would so intrigue eleven-year-olds that they would gladly jump into a sea of fractions? Food! I decided to ask the students to modify a recipe that serves six so that it could serve the entire class.

"I brought in a recipe today," I told them. "It's a recipe for trail mix. Do you know what trail mix is?" I was surprised when only a few students nodded. Kenneth raised his hand but retracted it as soon as he and I made eye contact.

Enrique spoke up. "It has nuts and berries."

"And raisins and little chocolate pieces," added Ramon.

Neal chimed in, "I think it has brown sugar."

"Okay," I said, "you know some of the ingredients. Can anyone guess why it's called trail mix?"

"You don't have to sit down to eat it," Jenny volunteered.

"Right," I agreed, "it's a snack that hikers and backpackers take with them on trips because it's easy to eat and healthy."

I put a transparency of the recipe (see the blackline master on the previous page) on the overhead and had Annabel read it aloud. When she had finished, I pointed to the last line. "It says, serves six. What does that mean?"

Chip jumped in. "It serves six people. If you make that recipe it's enough for six people to eat."

"Well," I responded, "what if we want to make enough trail mix for the whole class? How many people would we need to serve?" There was some disagreement here. First I needed to clarify that we would include children who were absent. Then we needed to decide whether to include their teacher and their student teacher. That narrowed it down to 32, 33, or 34 people. This debate was quite useful, because it gave me several numbers from which to choose.

I decided to go with 33 because "it's in the middle." My real reason was to learn how the students would deal with this "messy" number. How far could I push their computation and problem solving? They'd need to do some serious work to change a recipe from six servings to 33 servings. Or would some of the students convert the recipe to 36 servings and leave it at that? In the real world, this would be appropriate. If there is enough trail mix for 36 people, there certainly is enough for 33 people, with just a little left over. Would the students simplify the problem this way? I suspected that some would be quite satisfied with 36 servings while others would want to be more precise.

Not sure how difficult the task would be, and curious to see what approaches the students would use, I decided to have everyone work on one ingredient before we tackled the entire recipe. I pointed to the recipe projected on the overhead and indicated the half cup of raisins. "Okay," I said, "a half cup of raisins is what we need to serve six people. So we need to figure out how many cups of raisins we'll need to serve 33. Everyone will need a piece of paper and pencil to work on this problem. It might be very helpful to talk with the other people at your table as you think about this problem and work on it, but you each need to end up with a paper that shows your own thinking and work. I'll let you work on this for a while, and then we'll get back together and some of you will come to the overhead to show how you thought about it. Make sure your papers have the information you'd need to explain your thinking and how you got your answer."

I removed the recipe from the overhead and wrote on a clean transparency, *One-half cup raisins serves 6 people. How many cups will you need to serve 33 people?* "This is the problem you'll be working on at your tables. Are there any questions?"

Observing the Students

The students set to work. As I circulated, I noticed immediately that there was a range of comfort with the problem. Some students jumped right into the computation and were organizing their work in columns or rows. Other students were slower to engage.

Sometimes the biggest challenge is getting a student to articulate the task. I try to direct students to the task at hand through a series of questions, beginning with general ones I'm pretty sure they'll be able to answer. (I learned *How's it going?* from reading about Nancie Atwell's writers workshop. It's a nonthreatening, open-ended question that allows students to share what's on their mind without worrying that you're looking for something in particular.) Then I use these answers to ask more specific questions. It takes more time than if I simply repeated the problem or told them to get to work, but in order for children to develop their number sense, they need to construct their own understanding of the problem. Then they need to make mathematical decisions based on this understanding.

Many of the students in the class grasped the problem as I was leading the whole-class discussion and explaining the assignment. The problem meant something to them by the time we'd finished the introductory part of the activity. But, inevitably, there are students who get lost somewhere along the way. Today a few students were meticulously copying the question from the overhead. I needed to spend some time prompting these procrastinators. Ralph was one of them. "So, how's it going?" I asked him.

"Good," he answered.

"What are you working on?" I asked.

"We have to do the problem," he answered dutifully.

"What is the problem?" I asked.

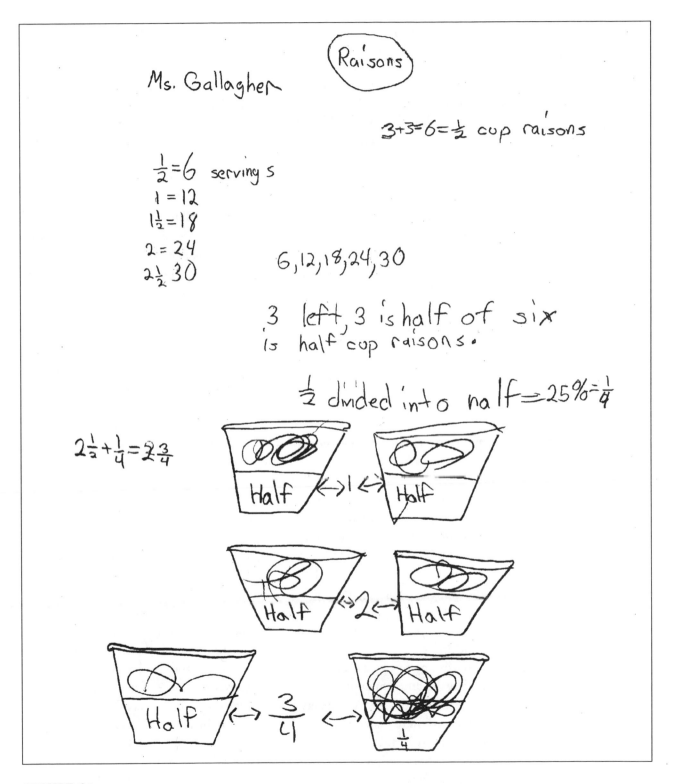

FIGURE 6.1

Howard's work on the raisins.

"Uh, it's a recipe."

"Yes," I responded, "and what are you supposed to do with the recipe?"

"We have to do thc raisins," Ralph continued.

I pointed to the question he had written on his paper. "Oh, so the recipe says a half cup of raisins serves six people. So, what are you supposed to do?"

Ralph seemed to brighten. "We have to do the raisins for the whole class."

"How do you think you can find that out?" I asked him.

Ralph gave that some thought and began to write on his paper:

$$^1/_2 = 6$$
$$1 = 12$$
$$1^1/_2 = 18$$

"I can do this and keep going until I get to 33," he told me.

"Great," I responded. I wondered what would happen when he realized he wouldn't get to 33 exactly. I decided not to confuse him by bringing it up. He understood the problem and was getting into the math, so I moved on. I let him continue working, making a mental note to see how he and other students using the same strategy dealt with the 33.

Continuing to circulate, I was amazed at the different approaches students took to the problem. Many students used more than one approach. Howard's paper included words, pictures, fractions, skip counting, and percents (see figure 6.1)!

I was surprised that most of the students dealt precisely with 33

servings. Very few of them were comfortable giving an "about" answer. Most of them did some sort of repeated addition or skip counting until they arrived at 30 or 36 servings. From there they struggled to split a serving of six in half and then add it to 30 or subtract it from 36. Had the students lost track of the context while working with the numbers? After all, we were talking about trail mix. Would anyone suffer if 33 people had to share a quantity sufficient for 30 people? Would there be a lot of waste if we made 36 servings for 33 people? At some point in the activity I would need to help them realize that in this context 30 servings or 36 servings would be close enough. At the moment, however, I was very interested in how the class dealt with the fractions and the fractions of fractions, so I let them work without questioning their excessive precision.

A Class Discussion

After the students had been working for about twenty minutes, I called them back together as a class. Some were still working on ways to organize their work. Others had found out the quantity of raisins needed for exactly 33 people and had begun to work on converting some of the other ingredients in the recipe. I was pleased the problem had enough richness to keep all students engaged at some level. It was an appropriate time to ask a few students to share their work. It could suggest some alternative approaches to those who were still struggling, and those who where working on the rest of the recipe would be introduced to other strategies and stretch their thinking.

"Who would like to come to the overhead and show the class how you approached this problem?" I asked. To emphasize the communication aspect of this report, I added, "If you're raising your hand, it means you're willing to come to the overhead and show us your thinking. You'll need to do it two ways. One way is to write on the overhead to give us an idea of what you did on your paper to help you solve the problem. The other part of the job is to talk to us about what you're writing on the overhead so we'll understand where your numbers and ideas came from. It's kind of tricky to write and talk at the same time, but it will really help us understand your thinking. Does anyone want to give it a try?"

There were quite a few eager volunteers. I called on Francine, writing her name at the top of a clean transparency. She took her paper from her desk, went to the overhead, picked up a pen, and went to work.

"Okay," she told us, " a half cup serves six people." She wrote on the overhead: $^1/_2$ *serves 6.* "So one half plus one half equals one whole, and that serves 12." Francine glanced at her paper and wrote:

$$^1/_2 + {}^1/_2 + 1 \; whole + {}^1/_2 + {}^1/_2 + {}^1/_2$$
$$6 + 6 = 12 + 6 + 6 + 6 = 30$$
$$25 = {}^1/_4$$

"See," she explained, "I just kept adding a half, and that's six more

people, and I kept going until I got to 30."

"Can you tell us about the 25 you wrote at the bottom?" I asked.

"Well," she responded, "I got to 30, but then if I added another one half, that would get me to 36, and I only want to get to 33. So I knew one half of one half is one fourth, and one fourth is 25 percent."

I was impressed and confused. I agreed with Francine's computation, but I didn't see where it got her in terms of solving the problem. "So how does the 25 percent help you with the recipe?" I asked.

Francine was honest. "I don't know. I got kind of confused after this part."

"This is a tough problem," I agreed. I didn't want to continue publicly questioning Francine about an idea that was still rather fragile. She had a partial understanding of the connection between fractions and percents, she had taken a risk and talked to her peers about her thinking, and I wanted her to remember it as a positive experience, not a time when she was put on the spot in front of the whole class. If I wanted to pursue the topic, a private discussion would be more appropriate.

Ramon came to the overhead next. Before he began speaking, he wrote:

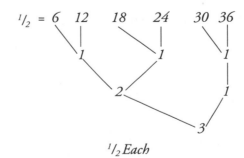

$^1/_2$ *Each*

"I counted by sixes, and each six is one-half cup," Ramon explained. "So then I drew lines to add the half cups together and make wholes. Then I added the wholes together, and it takes three cups."

Ramon was satisfied with converting the recipe to 36 servings. Did he know that 36 was close enough in the context of the problem, or had he been unsure how to deal with 33? I decided to ask. "So, Ramon, you figured out how to make enough trail mix for 36 people."

"Yep," he responded.

"I though we were trying to serve 33 people," I replied.

"Well," Ramon explained, "36 is really close to 33. If there's extra we can give some to our student teacher." Ramon had indeed used his number sense to realize that 36 was close enough to 33. "Uh-uh," interjected Shannon, "we already counted our student teacher in the 33."

"No we didn't," Kate disagreed.

Since we seemed on the verge of rehashing the original discussion of how many people were in the class, I cut the discussion short. "Whether or not you counted your student teacher, there would be enough trail mix if you made the recipe for 36, right?" I asked the class. It was hard to argue with that, and we were ready to move on.

Howard was the final volunteer before recess. "I wrote it down this way," he showed the class:

$$\frac{1}{2} = 6 \text{ servings}$$
$$1 = 12$$
$$1\frac{1}{2} = 18$$
$$2 = 24$$
$$2\frac{1}{2} = 30$$

"I just kept adding the halves on this side, and I added the sixes on the other side. Then I saw that two and a half cups serves 30 people. I wanted to get to 33, though. So I needed one half of a one half." He wrote on the overhead:

$$\frac{1}{2} \text{ divided by } \frac{1}{2} = \frac{1}{4}$$
$$\frac{1}{2} + \frac{1}{4} = \frac{3}{4}$$
$$2\frac{3}{4}$$

Howard seemed quite comfortable with the fractions. He had mentally taken one half of one half. He'd also added one fourth to one half with ease. This told me he had a level of fraction sense and was comfortable using "friendly" fractions. The only issue was his use of the term *divided* when describing how he found one half of one half. The class hadn't yet worked on multiplying or dividing fractions, so I wasn't concerned about his semantics. He had split a number ($\frac{1}{2}$) into two smaller, equal numbers ($\frac{1}{4}$ and $\frac{1}{4}$), and that matched his ideas about division more than multiplication.

"I'm very impressed with the work you've done so far," I told the class. "The next job will be finding out how much of the other ingredients we'll need for this recipe."

"I already know some of them!" exclaimed Enrique.

"Can we work on it for homework?" asked Latisha.

Pleased with their enthusiasm, I decided to let them try to convert some of the other ingredients as a homework assignment. I knew they would experience varying degrees of success, but I felt it would be beneficial for the students to "mess around" with some other fractions independently. I would use another whole-class period to discuss their work and come to a consensus on the rest of the recipe.

A Later Class Discussion

"I looked at your homework and the papers you did in class with me the last time I was here," I told the class a few days later. The night before I had gone through their papers (class work and homework) and categorized the different strategies students had used. I'd given the approaches names so we could refer to them in today's discussion. "I saw a lot of mathematical thinking. I also noticed that some of the fractions seemed kind of challenging to work with. Did anyone find a fraction that was challenging for you?"

Several hands went up. I called on Traci.

"I was trying to do the three-fourths cup of peanuts, and it was really hard. My brother couldn't even do it." (Traci's brother is in middle school.)

"Yes," I agreed, "I noticed that was a tough one for a lot of people. Were there any other fractions that were especially challenging?"

Chip jumped in. "Me and my mom tried to do the two-thirds cup of granola. It was hard, but we finally got it. Do you want me to tell you the answer?"

"Not yet," I responded. "We're going to take some time for you to work at your tables on the rest of these ingredients. Before you get to work, though, I want to show you some of the ways different people worked on this problem. It might be interesting and helpful for you to see some different strategies and tools people used. This is not an easy problem at all. You have to work with different fractions and think about ways to increase them so you'll have enough for 33 people. You have to keep track of a lot of numbers and stay organized as you work. There's a lot of math here. So, before you get back to work, I'm going to show you some approaches your classmates used. Maybe after you see some of these ideas, you'll have new ways to think about the problem. They may help you work on some of the fractions that were especially tricky."

I began with the most common approach. "I saw skip counting on quite a few papers," I told the class. On a projected transparency I wrote:

Skip Counting $^1/_2$ 1 $1^1/_2$ 2 $2^1/_2$ 3 . . .

"Some of you skip counted by fractions," I reported. "I also saw a lot of skip counting by sixes." I added this approach to the overhead:

Skip Counting   6   12   18   24 . . .

"Why would it be helpful to skip count by six?" I asked. I wanted to be sure the students were connecting the numbers I was writing to the problem. Emphasizing the relationship between the numbers and the problem gives the numbers meaning. The more meaning the numbers have, the more opportunities students have to deepen number sense.

"Because that's how many people," answered Enrique.

"Six people?" I asked.

"Yes," Jenny replied, "six people for each serving. The recipe serves six so you need to go by sixes when you make more."

"Okay," I said. "Another strategy I saw on some papers was a table." I wrote:

Amount	# of People
$^1/_2$	6
1	12
$1^1/_2$	18

I also showed examples of a picture strategy and a branching strategy.

"Take a few minutes at your tables now," I instructed the class. "Talk to your group members about these different strategies. Tell which strategies you used and which new ones you might want to try when you start working."

I allowed the groups several minutes to discuss their previous work and the approaches they had used. I wanted to reinforce two important ideas: there is more than one way to solve a problem, and listening to others can give you new ideas. Then I put the transparency of the recipe back on the overhead.

"Okay," I said, "the last time I was here you worked on the one-half cup of raisins, so that's done. The recipe also calls for one-half cup of dried fruit. That's pretty much the same problem as the raisins, so we

don't need to work on that one. That leaves us with four more ingredients to determine amounts for. Since there are eight tables of students, I'm going to assign each of the remaining ingredients to two tables. That way we can check to see whether the two tables agree on the answers." I assigned each table an ingredient, writing the ingredients and the table numbers on the board so we'd remember who was working on what.

I wanted to refocus on the context of the problem before I sent them off to do their work. "So," I asked, "who can remind us what we're trying to do here?" There were several volunteers. I called on Jon.

"We have to work with our groups to find out how much of our ingredient we need," he said.

"And how many people do we need to serve?" I asked innocently.

"Thirty-one."

"No. Thirty-two."

"No. It was 33."

"Marco and Annabel are absent."

"Julio was absent last time."

"We forgot to count our student teacher."

Clearly the problem had a real-world context. I had to get the class back to the original problem. "Well, I know some people are missing today who were here last time. It's good to realize that, but since we already started to change this to a 33-serving recipe, maybe we should stick with that number. If that's not exactly the number of people, there can be some sharing to even it out. We'll be close enough with 33."

Observing the Students

The students went to work, easily engaging in the problem. Their previous work and our introductory discussion probably helped. I noticed that several of the students employed more than one approach when working this time. Apparently, the display of different strategies had paid off, giving some of the students multiple ways to attack the problem. Juan used a table and a picture to

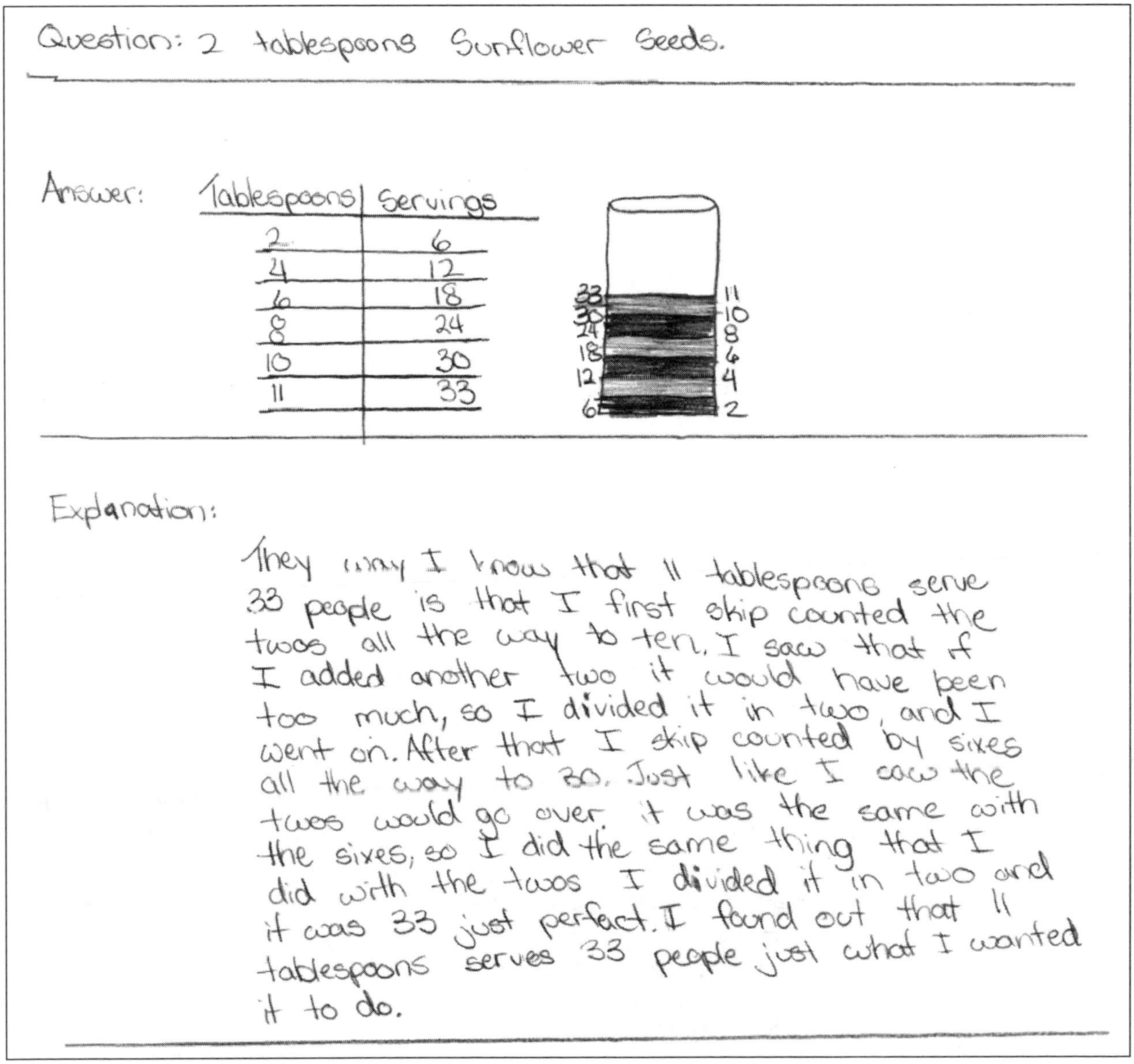

Question: 2 tablespoons Sunflower Seeds.

Answer:

Tablespoons	Servings
2	6
4	12
6	18
8	24
10	30
11	33

Explanation:

They way I know that 11 tablespoons serve 33 people is that I first skip counted the twos all the way to ten. I saw that if I added another two it would have been too much, so I divided it in two, and I went on. After that I skip counted by sixes all the way to 30. Just like I saw the twos would go over, it was the same with the sixes, so I did the same thing that I did with the twos I divided it in two and it was 33 just perfect. I found out that 11 tablespoons serves 33 people just what I wanted it to do.

FIGURE 6.2

Juan explained his sunflower seed solution.

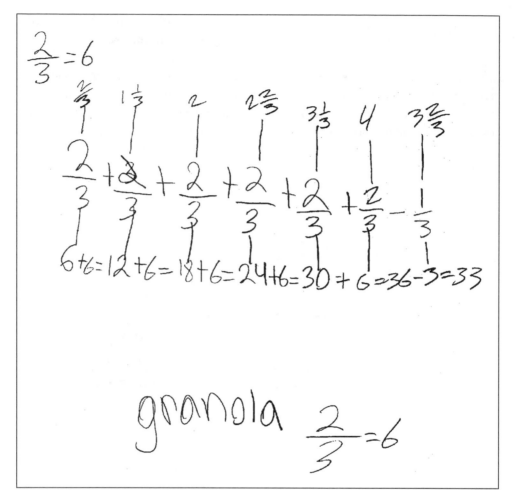

FIGURE 6.3
Raquel skip counted by ²/₃s.

calculate how many tablespoons of sunflower seeds were needed (see figure 6.2). Rachel used a combination of skip counting and branching to work on the granola (see figure 6.3).

Having more than one doorway through which to enter a problem allows for flexible thinking, which is a cornerstone of number sense. If children have a single procedure for doing a problem, they will invariably be stuck if they forget part of the

procedure or encounter a problem that is slightly different from the ones they're familiar with. Flexible thinkers can try a variety of angles and are more likely to find ways to solve the complicated problems encountered in real life.

A Class Discussion

I called the class back together after they had been working about twenty-five minutes. A reporter from each table told the class which ingredient they'd worked on and how much of it we'd need to serve 33 people. We found that the two tables working on the same ingredient agreed on their answers in most cases. Again, all tables had chosen to find the exact answer for 33 people rather than getting "close enough." The only controversial ingredient was the two-thirds cup of granola. The two tables working on granola did not get the same answer, so I had all the tables spend some time working and discussing this problem. Eventually consensus was reached. We had achieved our goal of converting a recipe that serves six to one that serves 33.

Extending the Activity

While I was impressed with these fifth graders' work and their ability to deal with fractions, I wasn't sure whether the students realized that if we were actually making trail mix, there would be no need for such precise measurements. I decided to devote a class period to estimation. I began with a story that I hoped would springboard into a discussion.

"I went to the grocery store this morning and I was thinking about that trail mix recipe. I was in the aisle that had granola, so I picked up a bag to look at. I remembered that for six people we needed two thirds of a cup. But I couldn't remember how much we needed for 33 people, so I started to work on the problem in my head. I

looked at how much granola was in the bag, thinking that might help me solve the problem. The bag said 33 ounces. Now I was really confused, because I wasn't sure how to compare ounces and two-thirds cups. Suddenly, I said to myself, Wait a minute—*it's trail mix.* So what if the amount of granola isn't exact? It will still taste fine. I can't ruin the recipe by having a little too much or a little less than I'm supposed to.

"My point is that I really didn't need to worry about exactly how much granola I needed to buy. I just needed to estimate and make sure I had about enough for 33 people. I only had to decide whether I needed one bag or two. I couldn't buy part of a bag even if I wanted to. I didn't need to know the answer to the fraction of a cup. Estimation was the key to solving my grocery store problem. I think estimation is the key to solving a lot of real-life math problems. Can anyone think of another example where you just need to estimate to get a close enough answer? And what about examples where you do need to be accurate?"

Several children raised their hand. I drew a table on the overhead and labeled one side "estimate" and the other side "accurate":

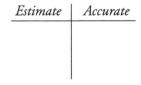

Estimate	*Accurate*

I put trail mix under the *estimate* category, and looked around for student suggestions.

"You need to be accurate with lasagna," Josue said. "You have to measure to make sure you don't put in too much sauce." I wasn't sure that veteran cooks would all agree. Often a good deal of estimating and eyeballing is involved in cooking. However, Josue seemed to be speaking from experience, so I decided to respect his precise cooking style. I put *lasagna sauce* in the *accurate* column.

Not wanting this to turn into a discussion solely about recipes, I tried to broaden the scope. "Let's try to get a list of real-life examples of when it's fine to estimate and when you need to be accurate. The ideas don't only have to be about food and recipes," I told the class, "try to think about different kinds of situations."

Kenneth jumped in. "I know," he announced. "When you go to the store to buy something, it has to be accurate."

"Yes," I agreed, "when I buy something I don't want the cashier to say, *Hmm, looks like about $30 dollars worth.*" I heard a number of chuckles. "Also," I added, "I don't think people at the store would appreciate it if I said, *Here's twenty dollars, that's about right.*" I put *shopping* in the *accurate* column.

We continued this whole-class discussion for a few more minutes and generated several more ideas for each side of the table.

A Writing Assignment

Then I gave the class an assignment. "Okay, each of you is going to get a piece of paper. You're going to make your own table and list real-life

examples of when you estimate and when you have to be more accurate. It's fine to talk to people at your table while you're working. That will probably help give you more ideas."

Observing the Students

The students set to work without any trouble. They engaged in animated discussions at their tables and were happy to share their ideas with me as I circulated.

Amanda talked about shoes. "With shoe size, you have to be accurate. If you don't have the right size, your shoes will fall off or be too tight."

Greg had written *medicine* under *accurate*. I asked him to explain. "You have to give the right amount of medicine. If a toddler is only supposed to have half a pill, you can't give him a whole pill, because he might get really sick."

Howard and Enrique were having a debate about homework assignments. "When you do your weekly report," said Howard, "you have to be accurate. You have to put down exactly how much you read."

Enrique shook his head. "I don't," he responded. "I don't count every single minute. I just read a lot."

"Well, I'm putting it down for accurate," Howard told Enrique.

"Fine," Enrique replied. "For me it's an estimate."

I eavesdropped on several similar discussions about clothing size, car mileage, and taxes. It wasn't important to me that the students come to a consensus on any particular item. I was just pleased that they were connecting real-life context to the important mathematical notions of estimation and accuracy. Their papers showed a wide range of examples (see figures 6.4 and 6.5).

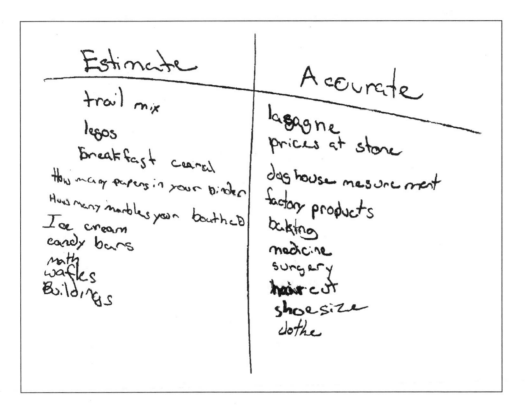

FIGURE 6.4

Examples of estimates versus accurate answers.

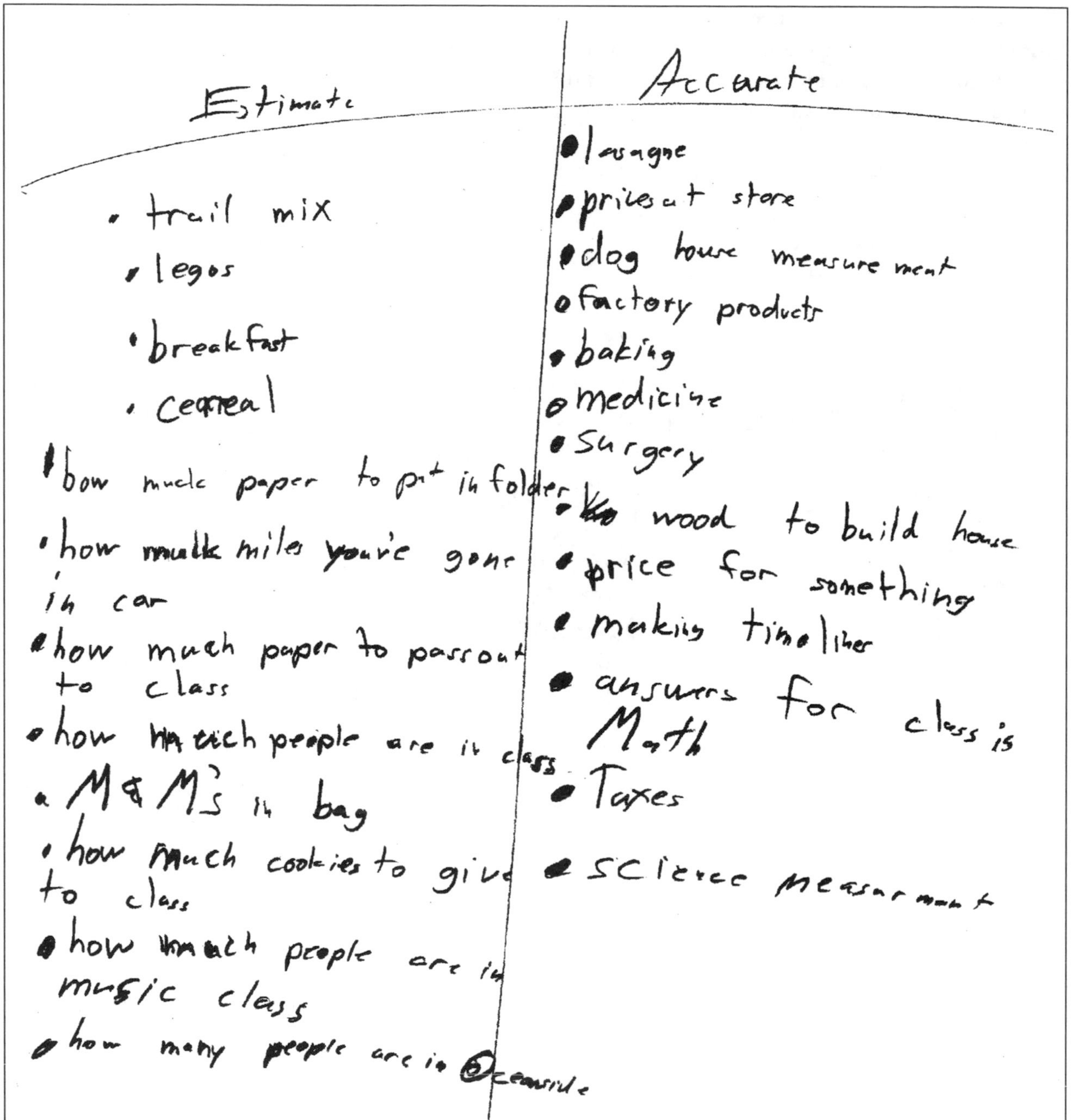

Estimate	Accurate
• trail mix	• lasagne
• legos	• prices at store
• breakfast	• dog house measurement
• cereal	• factory products
• how much paper to put in folder	• baking
• how much miles you're gone in car	• medicine
• how much paper to pass out to class	• surgery
• how much people are in class	• wood to build house
• M&M's in bag	• price for something
• how much cookies to give to class	• making timeliner
• how much people are in music class	• answers for class is Math
• how many people are in Oceanside	• Taxes
	• science measarment

FIGURE 6.5

More examples of estimates versus accurate answers.

CAREN ANSWERS YOUR QUESTIONS

What is the purpose of this activity?

This activity gives students a lot of experiences with fractions. They need to think about fractions, compare them, and convert them. They are asked to do quite a bit of computation. An important feature of the activity is the context it gives students for their work with fractions. The recipe format is interesting and gets students to think about fractions in a meaningful way, thus helping them develop their number sense.

Isn't it risky to assign a homework problem that is very challenging? What if students can't do it?

It would be frustrating and pointless to assign a challenging homework problem that isn't followed up in class. However, this assignment is a piece of a bigger mathematical investigation; it doesn't stand alone. It's another chance for students to think about fractions and methods for converting the recipe. Whether or not students are wholly successful at home, they come to class with a little more experience to build from. Even if a student has not done the homework, which happens, listening to others' ideas and experiences is beneficial.

What is the point of having students talk at their tables and then write individually?

The student discussions are a "pre-writing" activity. It may seem that by having students talk, they are telling one another the answer. However, with a complex problem, the cross-pollination of ideas doesn't taint the individual products. Rather, the talk lets individuals focus on what they understand and gives them different ways to think about the problem.

After the discussion, when students write independently, they can only draw from what they have internalized. Although what they have heard may provide some mental resources, both in terms of ideas and words with which to express the ideas, the ideas on the paper are nevertheless their own. (If they aren't, it's usually pretty obvious.)

How can this activity be used to assess students' number sense?

I had many chances to assess the students throughout the activity. The following questions helped me frame my assessment of a student's number sense:

- Which ingredients were relatively easy for students to convert?
- Which were more challenging?
- What computational procedures did students employ to convert the fractions?

- How did students organize their paper to help them see and make sense of the fractions?
- Which students were eager to share their thinking with the whole class?
- Which students tried new approaches after hearing their classmates talk about them?
- Were students able to clearly express their ideas in writing?

Why did you have the students spend time on the accurate/ estimate discussion?

I felt it would be very worthwhile. Many of the students had been very concerned about determining a precise answer for each trail mix ingredient. I wanted to broaden their perspective. In reality, many problems do not call for an exact answer. In order to build number sense it's important for students to have opportunities to estimate and opportunities to be precise. To further build number sense, students need to work on problems that have a real-world context so they'll be able to make the decision about how precise an answer needs to be. By discussing these ideas, students will be more likely to consider the estimate/ accurate alternative when solving future problems.

Navigating the Number System

*I*n addition to becoming comfortable with numerical operations, students need experiences that give them a broader understanding of our base ten number system, a system that consists of very orderly patterns and consistent characteristics. For example, we expect students to know, without using paper and pencil or a calculator, what happens when ten is added to a number or when a number is multiplied by ten. Understanding the importance of tens in our number system gives students access to many computational strategies. Similarly, students need to recognize the patterns inherent to odd and even numbers, factors, and multiples.

If children are aware of the structure and patterns behind our number system, they are able to understand relationships among numbers and can predict and evaluate reasonable solutions to math problems. This deeper understanding and the ability to predict are essential components of number sense.

Teachers play a critical role in guiding students' learning about the number system. The key is to give students many opportunities to negotiate the system, letting them chart their own course through familiar territory and challenging them to discover and investigate new paths along the way.

In the four activities in this section, students will read, write, talk, and make computations in order to learn about and understand the infrastructure of our number system. Each activity focuses on getting students to think about and use numbers in ways that make sense to them.

7

Numbers and Me

Overview

Learning to see the usefulness of numbers is an important part of developing number sense. In this activity students identify some "personal numbers"—numbers that describe them or relate to their life in some way. For example, 132 might be the number of a student's house in his street address; 52 might be her height in inches; $11\frac{1}{2}$ might be his age. Then they play a guessing game with another student in which they try to match the numbers with the things to which the numbers refer. The activity can provide experience with whole numbers, fractions, decimals, and percents.

Teaching Directions

1. On the chalkboard or a projected transparency, write between ten and fifteen numbers that have some significance to your life.

2. Give a clue about each number (for example, *One of these numbers stands for the number of years I've been teaching* or *One of these numbers stands for the number of miles on my car*) and ask the students to decide which number best suits each clue.

3. Have the students write down on a sheet of paper ten or fifteen numbers that have some significance in their life. On a separate piece of the paper, ask them to write a sentence that describes each number. For example:

1987	This is the year in which I was born.
3	This is the number of siblings I have.
$33\frac{1}{3}$	This is the percentage of the day I spend sleeping.
$\frac{1}{2}$	This is the portion of our class that are girls.

4. Have the students, in pairs, exchange their lists of numbers, then take turns reading their clues (at random) and guessing which number fits which clue.

IN THE CLASSROOM WITH RUSTY

Introducing the Activity

Since Pam Long was preparing to teach her fifth graders a unit on fractions, decimals, and percents, I thought Numbers and Me would not only be a way to assess students' understanding of these concepts but also give them opportunities to develop their number sense.

To begin the activity, I wrote these numbers on the chalkboard: $33\frac{1}{3}$; 190; 4; 10; 2614; $42\frac{2}{3}$; .25; 558,903,281; 6,192,837,065; 17; $66\frac{2}{3}$; 3; 12,658; 29; 1954; and 134,155. "The numbers on the board are my personal numbers," I told the class. "They all have something to do with my life. They have meaning to me."

"What do they stand for?" asked Britt.

"That's one of the things you're going to figure out today," I said. "I'll read you clues about the numbers and see whether you can guess what the numbers stand for. First, I'd like you to read the numbers silently." I waited while the students read the numbers to themselves. "Raise your hand if you'd like to read this number," I said, as I pointed to the number 1954. I called on Jaime and I used my index finger to point to the digits as he read them aloud.

"One thousand nine hundred fifty-four," he read. When he finished, I directed the class to read the number together and again I pointed to the digits.

"Who'd like to read this number?" I asked, pointing to 134,155. I called on Mary.

"Thirteen thousand four hundred and . . . ," Mary began. She stopped and looked puzzled, then tried again. "One hundred thirty-four thousand?" she asked hesitantly.

"That's right," I confirmed. "How do you finish reading the number?"

"One hundred thirty-four thousand one hundred fifty-five," Mary said more confidently. After she finished, I asked the class to read the number out loud together.

"Who would like to read this number?" I then asked the class, pointing to .25.

"I think it's point 25," said Mary. "The point is a decimal point."

"Another way is 25 hundredths," said Tom.

"It's like 25 cents or part of a dollar," added Ronesha.

We read the rest of the numbers on the chalkboard aloud. I had to help the class read the two largest numbers; the one in the billions gave everybody trouble. When we were finished, I continued with the activity. "Now I'll read you clues about my numbers. Listen while I read and see whether you can guess which number I'm describing. It's important that you're respectful when you guess numbers. For example, if I said that one of the numbers is how old I am and you guessed 190, that might hurt my feelings." The students giggled. "I know a guess like that would be funny, but it's important not to hurt people's feelings on purpose," I said. Students nodded their head in agreement.

"Here's my first clue," I said. *"This is the year in which I was born."* Many hands shot up, with lots of oohs and ahs. "I believe I'll call on someone who is being silent," I said. As the students quieted down, more hands were raised. I called on Rose.

"It's nineteen fifty-four!" she exclaimed.

"When Jaime read the number aloud, he said it was one thousand nine hundred and fifty-four," I said. "Why did you read it differently?"

"Because that's how you read numbers when it's a year," she explained.

"How did you know that I was born in 1954?" I asked.

"Because all the years in this century begin with 19," she replied. "That gave it away for me."

"Okay," I said. "You know the year in which I was born. Can you use that information to help you figure out which number stands for my age?" A few students raised their hand immediately, but I gave the class some time to think about this question. Then I called on Amy.

"I think you're 42 and two-thirds years old," said Amy.

"Why do you think that?" I asked.

"Well, I don't think you're 79," she said with a giggle. "I know I'm supposed to be nice, so sorry I'm laughing."

"That's okay," I responded. "I'm glad you're reminding us."

Amy smiled and continued. "And all the other numbers don't fit your age, except maybe 33 and one third," she said. Amy understood that most of the numbers on the board didn't make

sense when thinking about my age. Recognizing the suitability of numbers is part of having number sense. Some numbers are appropriate for some things but not for others.

"Did anyone think about this in a different way?" I asked.

"I wrote 1997 minus 1954 on my paper and got 43," Miguel reported. "But there's no 43 on the board."

"I think your birthday's coming up and then you'll be 43, but you're still 42," offered Betsabe.

"I am 42 and two-thirds years old," I said. "Can someone explain what the two thirds means?" I waited several seconds, then called on Reba.

"The fraction means part of a year," she said.

"That's correct," I replied. "In this case, the fraction means part of a year. It's the amount of time that's passed since my last birthday, which was in October."

"I think the two thirds stands for two thirds of a year, which is eight months, because there's twelve months in a year and three fours in twelve," Courtney reasoned.

"Does that make sense?" I asked the class. While a few students nodded in agreement, others seemed lost. I decided they needed more time to grapple with what two thirds meant in this situation.

"I want you to talk to the person next to you about what two thirds means if I'm 42 and two-thirds years old," I said. After a moment, I called them back to attention and again posed the question.

"If you count the months from October till the end of this month, you'll get eight months," Jason explained. "November, December, January, February, March, April, May, June. You have four more months to go before you're 43. So eight months out of twelve months is like eight twelfths, and that's the same as two thirds."

"It's two thirds, because in a year you have three groups of four and you're 42 and two thirds or two fours out of three fours," Jessica added.

"Just make twelve tally marks on the board," suggested Betsabe. I drew the tally marks on the chalkboard. "Okay, the tally marks stand for the twelve months of the year," she explained. "Circle every four tally marks. There's three groups of four tally marks and two of the groups are circled. That's how you can see the two thirds of a year."

"All of these explanations make sense to me," I said. Continuing with the next clue, I read, *"This number represents how many brothers and sisters are in my family.* Look at the numbers on the board and think about which ones would fit," I instructed.

"Well, I think four and three and ten could be the answer," Tom said. "Maybe seventeen, but that would be a lot of sisters and brothers!"

"I have three siblings," I stated. "One of the numbers on the chalkboard tells what portion of us are boys. Raise your hand if you have an idea."

"It's point 25," said Miguel.

"Are you sure?" I asked, pushing for an explanation to check for understanding.

"Yeah," he said, "it's the same as

25 cents and that's like one fourth of a dollar."

"Can anyone add to what Miguel just said?" I asked.

"It's like one out of four are boys, or one fourth," answered Claire.

"Or 25 percent," added Gorgé.

I wrote *.25,* $^1/_4$, and 25% on the chalkboard. "So what percent of my brothers and sisters, including me, are girls?" I continued.

"Seventy-five percent!" several students chorused.

I wrote *.75* and *75%* on the chalkboard. "How do I write a fraction that means the same as 75 percent?" I asked, encouraging them to make another connection between decimals, percents, and fractions.

"Three fourths!" the students responded. I wrote $^3/_4$ on the chalkboard next to *.75* and *75%,* then continued with the next clue.

"This number represents the percent of the day I spend sleeping," I read. At first, few hands were raised. The students were studying the numbers and discussing them in their groups. I quickly toured the room, listening to their conversations. When I asked for their attention, I posed the same question but used different wording. "If you think of the numbers on the board as percents, what percent of the day might I spend asleep? Remember, when I say *day,* I'm including all 24 hours."

"I think you spend 33 and a third percent of the day sleeping," said Paula.

"Why do you think that?" I asked.

"Because if you spent 79 percent or 66 and two thirds percent sleeping, you'd be sleeping a lot!" she exclaimed.

"You could spend 17 percent of the day asleep," José offered.

"Or ten percent, but that would mean you weren't getting enough rest!" added Betsabe. Everyone laughed.

"Yes, I spend about 33 and a third percent of the day asleep," I confirmed. Judging by their responses, I wasn't sure that students understood how many hours $33^1/_3$ percent represented. I decided to ask a probing question to find out. "Do you think I spend more or less than 12 hours asleep? I want you to talk with someone at your table about this question." After a moment, I asked for the students' attention and called on Juan.

"You sleep less than 12 hours," he said.

"How do you know?" I asked.

"I don't know, I just think that," he replied.

"It's important that you're able to explain your thinking," I told the class. "I may agree with you, Juan, but I'm curious about how you figured the answer."

"It's because there are 24 hours in a day, okay?" Reba began. "So half of that is 12, and you said you sleep 33 and a third percent of the day, and that's less than half."

"What percent would be the same as half of the day?" I asked.

"Fifty!" the students chorused.

"So which number on the board tells what percent of the day I stay awake?" I asked. Almost every hand was raised. I called on Mary.

"Sixty-six and two thirds," she answered. "It's because that number

plus 33 and a third make 100 percent. A hundred percent means the whole day."

"I agree that 100 percent means a whole day," I said. "What about the numbers that are larger than 100? Could we use 190 as a percent?" A few students didn't think so, but most seemed perplexed. I knew this question was going to be difficult for them to think about. Sometimes I'll throw in a question like this to test the waters and see how far I can go with a concept. "Sometimes percents greater than 100 make sense, depending on the situation," I said. "For instance, sometimes the price of food or the cost of a house increases more than 100 percent." I stopped there, knowing that I'd probably reached the edge of their understanding about percents. "The next number is the age of my car," I said.

"The answer could be three, ten, or 17 years," said José. No one else raised a hand.

"I'll give you another clue," I told them. "The number on the board that represents the number of miles on my car is 134,155."

"How about three years?" Tawny guessed.

"That can't be!" Reba exclaimed. "We have a new car and it has about 10,000 miles on it."

"I think your car is 17 years old," said José.

"The only other number that works is ten years old," added Miguel.

"You're right," I said. "I bought my car when I started teaching in Oceanside, exactly ten years ago."

When the students had guessed

most of my personal numbers, I explained the directions for the next part of the activity. "You've guessed most of the numbers on the chalkboard. Now I'd like you to think of numbers that are special to you. I'd like you to write down as many numbers that you can think of that relate to you and then write clues about your numbers."

"I don't get the clues part," said Tom.

"You're going to write clues about your numbers, just like I gave you," I explained. "For example, if one of my numbers is 42 and two thirds, my clue might be: *This number tells how old I am.*" I wrote the number and the clue on the chalkboard as an example. "If one of my numbers is ten, I might write: *This is the number that tells the age of my car.*" Again I wrote the number and next to it the clue for students to see.

"Can we draw pictures?" asked Mary.

"That would be fine, as long as you also write a sentence that describes your number," I replied.

"How many numbers and sentences do we have to write?" asked Lydia.

"That's up to you," I said. "I think you should try to think of as many numbers as you can. Remember, the numbers should have something to do with your life. If you get stuck, talk with your partner."

I passed out paper, and the students eagerly began to write down their numbers. One student realized she could ascertain her height using the measuring tape against the wall,

then use that as one of her numbers. Soon, there was a line of students waiting to measure their height.

The students were excited about the activity and worked for the rest of the math period. For homework that night, I asked students to finish writing their numbers and their clues. I told them it was important that they bring their papers back the next day.

Observing the Students

The next day I gave the students about ten minutes at the beginning of math class to look over their numbers and their clues and add any necessary finishing touches. As I walked around the room watching and listening, I was impressed by the variety of ways in which students thought about numbers. (Figures 7.1 and 7.2 are two examples of students' personal numbers.)

Some students wrote about numbers that represented the dates of important events in their lives. Jim wrote down the year that he first got braces. Gwen wrote down the year she got her favorite bike. Tom recorded the year when he'll be 21 years old.

Many students were able to use fractions in meaningful ways. Rich wrote that three sevenths is the fraction that represents the portion of aunts he has on his mom's side of the family. Leu included two fractions that were linked. In his clue about $12/34$, he wrote: *This is the fraction of our class that's in band.* For $22/34$ he wrote: *This is the fraction of the class that isn't in band.* Linda used her height, five feet eight-

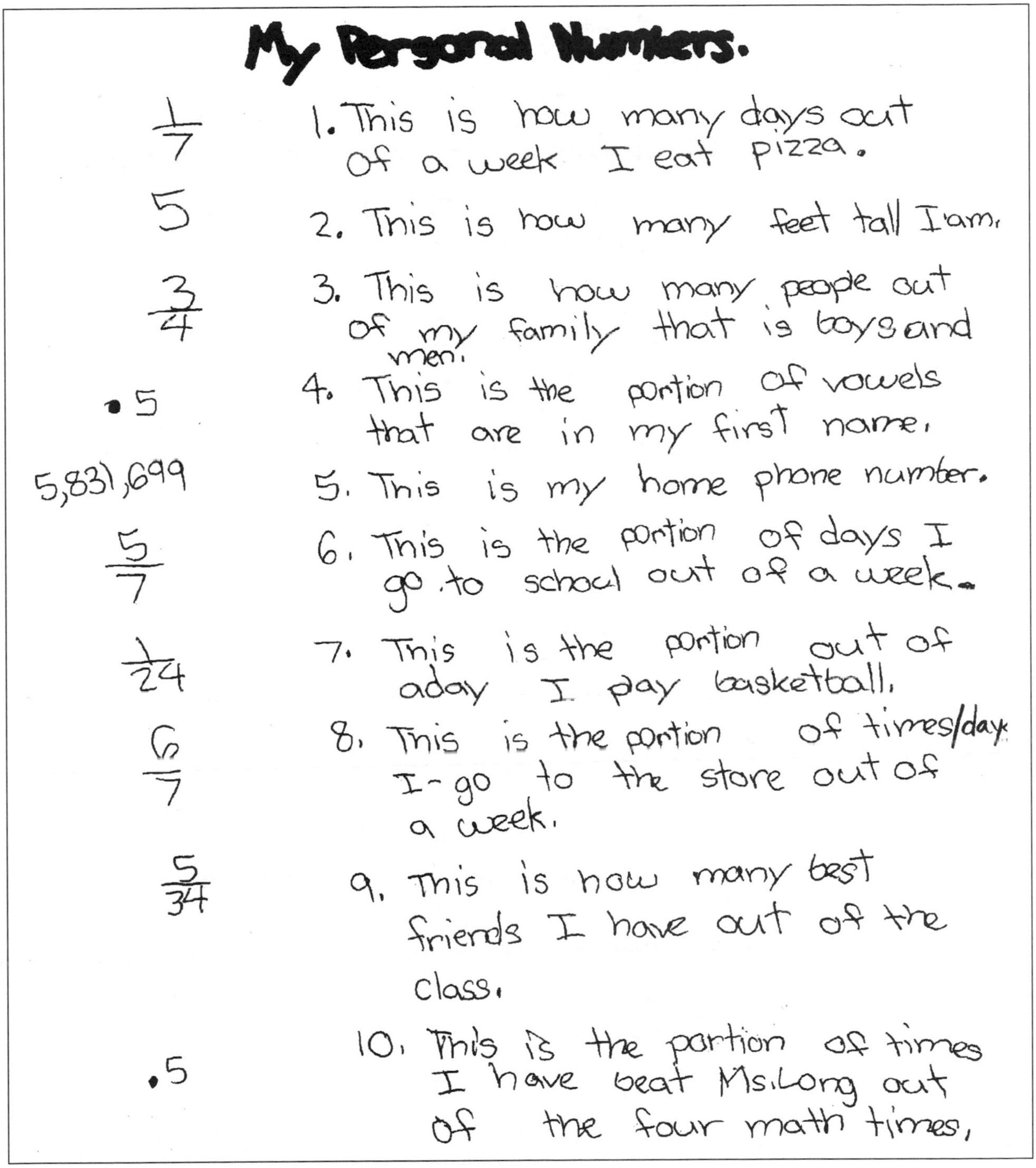

My Personal Numbers.

$\frac{1}{7}$ 1. This is how many days out of a week I eat pizza.

5 2. This is how many feet tall I am.

$\frac{3}{4}$ 3. This is how many people out of my family that is boys and men.

•5 4. This is the portion of vowels that are in my first name.

5,831,699 5. This is my home phone number.

$\frac{5}{7}$ 6. This is the portion of days I go to school out of a week.

$\frac{1}{24}$ 7. This is the portion out of a day I pay basketball.

$\frac{6}{7}$ 8. This is the portion of times/day I-go to the store out of a week.

$\frac{5}{34}$ 9. This is how many best friends I have out of the class.

.5 10. This is the portion of times I have beat Ms. Long out of the four math times.

FIGURE 7.1

José used mostly fractions to describe things in his life.

1,987	This number was the year I was born
.5	This number is the portion of girls in my family
$\frac{4}{5}$	This number is the portion of cousins that are girls in my family
$\frac{1}{2}$	this number is the portion of animals that are cats in my family
.5	This number is the portion of "A's in my first name
4,308,133	this number is my phone number
$\frac{1}{3}$	This number is the portion of male teachers I had at this school
5	This number is the letters in my dogs name
20	This number is the amount off Books I can read in a year

FIGURE 7.2

Amy thought about numbers in a variety of ways.

——

twelfths inches, as one of her personal numbers. Students used fractions in a variety of ways, including months in a year, days in a week, states in the union, kids in the class, and inches in a foot.

Some students made important connections between fractions and decimals. Jenny used two numbers to describe her age: 10.5 or $10^1/_2$. Maryanna, describing .5, wrote: *When I was 9 years old, I drew 50 pictures and*

I only like half of them. Which number means the same as $^1/_2$?

Students used 100 percent to describe the amount of time our heart beats, how much of the time we breathe, and the score on a test. And they used decimals to describe how much they paid for things, like Nintendo games.

Not all students had an easy time writing their clues. For example, some had difficulty writing large numbers correctly, and I spent time showing them where to place the commas in numbers like 7,545,483. Others struggled with how to describe fractions. One student wrote that $^1/_2$ represented the number of sisters in his family. When he realized that he didn't have half of a sister, he laughed and rewrote the clue this way: *$^1/_2$ represents the portion of my brothers and sisters that are sisters.* This difficulty with describing what the numbers meant was common and made me realize how important the role of language is in math class.

A Class Discussion

When all the students had finalized their papers, I called for their attention. "Today we're going to play a guessing game with our personal numbers, like I did with you yesterday," I began. "Yesterday I wrote my personal numbers on the chalkboard, then I read a sentence that told about one of the numbers and you guessed which number fit the sentence. The sentences were like clues. Who would like to volunteer to write your numbers on the chalkboard and read your clues to the class?"

The students were eager to share, and many hands shot up. I called on Emma. She walked to the front of the class and carefully wrote these numbers on the board: *1987; 3,850,684; 2; 122,889; .5; $^1/_3$; $^{17}/_{30}$; 30; $^7/_{24}$; 9,417,826.* "Remember, Emma, when you read a clue, don't give away the number that you're describing," I reminded her. "Read one clue at a time and let's see if someone can guess which number fits."

"Okay, this number is the year I was born," Emma said. Lots of hands raised. She called on Jenny.

"That's easy," said Jenny. "It's 1987. That's also the year I was born."

Emma smiled, then continued with her clues. "Okay, this number is the portion of our class that are girls." It was obvious that Emma enjoyed being the "teacher." She smiled as she scanned the room, looking for someone to call on. Finally she chose Rich.

"Is it point five?" he asked.

"Yes, that's it," Emma replied. "I used it because it means the same as one half, and half of our class are girls."

"If you wanted to use a percent for one half, what number would that be?" I interjected, taking the opportunity to help students make a connection between fractions, decimals, and percents. Drawing out the mathematics during classroom discussions is an important part of the teacher's role.

"That would be 50 percent," she replied.

"Could any other of Emma's numbers represent the portion of girls in our class?" I asked. I called on Alexa.

"Well, seventeen 30ths would be close if there were 30 kids in our class," she said. "Fifteen 30ths is one half, so that's pretty close."

Emma continued sharing her clues. "This is the number of hours I'm at the gym on Mondays." Lots of hands shot up. The students seemed sure about this answer.

"It's two," said Katrina. "No other numbers would work, except for point five, and you already used that." Katrina was thinking about the reasonableness of the available numbers in this situation.

Emma delivered her next clue. "This number represents how many hours I play outside on a weekend day." This time, everyone raised their hand. Emma called on Tamika.

"It's seven 24ths," said Tamika, smiling confidently.

"How did you know the answer?" I asked.

"It's easy," Tamika replied. "There's 24 hours in a day, and Emma plays seven hours out of 24." Tamika made sense of the numerator and denominator in this fraction.

Emma continued to read her clues to the class until the students had matched all the numbers to her clues. We continued to play the guessing game until the end of the math period as different students shared their numbers and clues. The following day, Pam continued the activity with her class, asking pairs of students to guess each other's clues.

RUSTY ANSWERS YOUR QUESTIONS

How will this activity help my students develop number sense?

Numbers and Me helps students develop their number sense in several important ways. First, it prompts them to think about the reasonableness of a number in a given situation. Students have to consider a variety of numbers in the context of any given clue: they need to think logically and eliminate numbers that don't fit. Next, the activity also provides a larger context for thinking about numbers, one outside the confines of the classroom. Students see that numbers are meaningful and can be used in a variety of ways, including to quantify, to label, to measure, and to locate. Providing a meaningful context helps students understand what numbers mean, whether they're fractions, decimals, percents, or whole numbers.

Why did you use your own personal numbers to start the activity?

There are a couple of reasons. First, I needed numbers to model the activity, so the students could connect my verbal directions to a specific example. Second, I wanted students to see that numbers are important and meaningful to me. I deliberately chose numbers that would engage the children in a variety of ways: I wanted them to think about large numbers, small numbers, decimal numbers, fractions, and numbers that represented percents.

What is the primary focus of the activity?

The primary focus is for students to think about numbers and relate them to familiar contexts. Number sense is characterized by the ability to make sense of numerical situations. I also wanted students to see that numbers that are appropriate for some situations may be inappropriate for others. Often, students are only asked to think about numbers in very specific ways—when doing arithmetic operations, for example. I wanted to give students an opportunity to have a conversation that would give them a "feel" for numbers.

During the activity, I deliberately kept the focus on discussing the meaning of numbers in context and away from teaching specific rules or procedures. For example, during our discussion the students grappled with the number $42^2/_3$, which represented my age. When I asked the students to think about what the two thirds meant, my intent was simply to give the students a context in which to think about fractions. Context diverts children from rules and procedures and encourages them to explore ideas in a more open and informal manner. In this activity I wanted the students to see that fractions have meaning in the real world. Understanding what numbers mean is at the heart of number sense.

Courtney seemed to understand that the two thirds in the number $42^2/_3$ represented eight months out of a year. What about the students who didn't follow her thoughts?

I know that during class discussions, not all the students are following or understanding what is being explained. Some discussions are most beneficial to the student doing the explaining. Courtney had a chance to clarify her ideas and cement her understanding: "I think the two thirds stands for two thirds of a year, which is eight months, because there's twelve months in a year and three fours in twelve." While a number of students then contributed similar explanations, others seemed lost or confused. I often worry about these students on the periphery. Are they daydreaming? Are they lost? What are they absorbing from the discussion? At times like this I shift gears and ask the students to talk to a neighbor in order to get another perspective or to voice their confusion. If I have time, I'll privately approach a student who I think is confused and ask more questions. Giving students the time to talk about numbers and their meaning helps them develop their number sense.

What are some ways to assess an individual student's number sense?

There are many ways to assess whether or not a student has a well-developed sense of numbers. In this activity, I kept several questions in mind as I observed the students in action:

- What numbers do students choose for their number clues? Do they choose only whole numbers? Are they comfortable using decimals? percents? fractions?
- What's the range of the numbers the students choose? Do they choose only small numbers or do they use large numbers as well?
- When students are playing the game with a partner, are they guessing suitable numbers after being given a clue? Do the students know whether other numbers fit the clue?
- When writing their clues, are students using a variety of contexts for their numbers? What kinds of contexts are they using?

- Are students having a difficult or an easy time relating numbers to contexts?

How can I do the activity without using personal numbers?

The activity can easily be adapted for other areas of the math curriculum. In a unit on measurement, for example, students can write number clues about different objects in the classroom: *size 9, 6 feet tall, 3 feet by 5 feet, 11 pounds,* etc. The activity can also be used in other subject areas. Students in a fifth-grade social studies class, for example, might use important numbers in U.S. history, such as 13 (for the 13 original colonies) and 1776.

8 *All About 1,000*

Overview

The number 1,000 is an important and useful landmark in our number system and is a benchmark for comparing numbers. This activity focuses students on thinking about 1,000 in various contexts. Students talk about what they know about the number, then listen to the book *How Much, How Many, How Far, How Heavy, How Long, How Tall Is 1,000?* After listening to the story, students develop their own questions about 1,000 related to a topic of their choice.

Materials Needed

A copy of the children's book *How Much, How Many, How Far, How Heavy, How Long, How Tall Is 1,000?,* by Helen Nolan, with illustrations by Tracy Walker (Kids Can Press, 1995).

Teaching Directions

1. Ask the students what they know about the number 1,000 and record their ideas.

2. Read aloud the book *How Much, How Many, How Far, How Heavy, How Long, How Tall Is 1,000?*

3. Review some of the topics addressed in the book, and ask students to suggest other topics in which they are interested.

4. Choose an example topic and have students brainstorm questions related to this topic that involve the number 1,000.

5. Ask each student to choose one topic and write down several questions related to that topic that involve the number 1,000.

6. Have each student explore one of their questions, first estimating the answer, then finding an accurate answer.

Example Questions for the Topic *Money*

If you laid 1,000 pennies end to end, about how long would that be? How much would 1,000 one-dollar bills weigh? If you earned $1.00 every minute, how many hours would it take to earn a $1,000?

All About 1,000

101

IN THE CLASSROOM WITH RUSTY

Introducing the Activity

"This week we're going to investigate the number 1,000," I told Maryann Wickett's fourth graders. "Understanding what numbers mean is important to our math thinking. I want you to close your eyes and think about what you know about the number 1,000." After several seconds, I asked the students to open their eyes and tell someone next to them what they were thinking. When they were finished, I asked the students to share their thoughts with the class.

"It has three zeros," said Benjamin.

"Let's check," I said. I wrote *1,000* on the chalkboard, and we counted the number of zeros to confirm Benjamin's statement.

"You can call it ten hundred," said Alexa.

"Let's count by 100s to see if what Alexa says is true," I told the class. Together we counted by 100 ten times.

"One thousand is a big number!" exclaimed Suzanne.

"One thousand is a four-digit number," said Mike.

"One thousand comes out in money," Zach reported.

"Tell us more, Zach," I probed.

"Like 1,000 dollars," he clarified. "On the show *America's Funniest Home Videos* they give the winner 1,000 dollars."

"It's an even number," added Jellian.

"How do you know?" I asked.

(Correct answers are often misleading. Asking probing questions gives me an insight into my students' number sense.)

"Because it has four digits," she responded.

"What about this number?" I said, writing *1,001* on the chalkboard. "This is a four-digit number, but it's odd. I only have to give one counterexample to disprove your theory. Other ideas about why 1,000 might be even?"

"One thousand is even because 999 is odd and it comes right before it," said Asha.

"So you think numbers alternate between odd and even?" I asked. Asha nodded yes.

"It's even because you can cut it in half evenly, half of 1,000 is 500," explained Isaiah.

"I think I'm convinced that 1,000 is an even number," I said with a smile. "What else can you say about 1,000?"

"One thousand has 200 fives in it," said Jan.

"How do you know?" I asked.

"Well, it takes 20 fives for 100, and there's ten 100s in 1,000, so you times 20 by ten and you get 200 fives," she explained. Jan's reasoning was solid and demonstrated an understanding of how numbers are put together.

After everyone who wished to had volunteered what she or he knew about 1,000, I gathered the students on the rug and held up the book *How Much, How Many, How Far, How Heavy, How Long, How Tall Is 1,000?* "In this book, the author asks lots of questions that have to do with 1,000,"

I said. "I'm going to read the story, and then I'll ask you some questions about the number 1,000."

The students listened attentively to the book's conjectures about what 1,000 looks like in different contexts (they also enjoyed the illustrations, which I held up as we went along): *What do 1,000 dandelions look like? What about 1,000 acorns in a pile? How about a forest of 1,000 oak trees? One thousand people sitting in rows would fill a small hockey arena. What would 1,000 people waiting in line to get in look like?*

When I got to the page that reads, *How much is 1,000? Is it a lot?*, I said to the class, "The author says that when it comes to hair on your head, 1,000 isn't very many. When isn't 1,000 a lot?" Their ideas didn't flow easily at first; it took time. There were many silent moments. But I wanted students to get an idea of the relative size of 1,000.

"If you have 1,000 pieces of grass," said Pat. I recorded Pat's idea on a piece of chart paper under the heading *1,000 Isn't a Lot* and added to the list as other students volunteered their thoughts.

"How about 1,000 atoms or electrons? That would be teeny tiny!" said Jellian, exaggerating the words *teeny tiny.*

"A thousand feathers wouldn't weigh very much," added Asha.

"Or 1,000 little ants or cookie crumbs," said Christopher.

"The book says that if you don't like freckles, 1,000 is a lot. When is 1,000 a lot?" I asked.

"It's a lot if you have 1,000 dollars!" Mike exclaimed. I wrote

1,000 Is a Lot at the top of another piece of chart paper and recorded Mike's idea underneath.

"How about 1,000 headaches!" cried Susan. Everyone giggled.

"If you owned 1,000 TVs, that would be a lot," said Sagan.

"One thousand volcanoes erupting would be scary and a lot!" exclaimed Joe.

"One thousand years is a long time and 1,000 seconds isn't," Alma observed.

I continued reading the book. When I got to the page with a picture of a girl, a boy, and their dog eating lots of french fries, I held it up. *"What about 1,000 french fries? Could you eat all of them?"* I quoted. "The author says a single serving has about 40 fries. How many friends would 1,000 french fries feed?" I wrote *40* on the chalkboard and asked the children to think about this and talk to someone next to them. Although the problem was too difficult for most of these beginning fourth graders to solve mentally, hearing estimates and plans for solving the problem would expose students to lots of ways of thinking about the problem and give me insight into their thinking about numbers and operations. After a moment or two, I called the class back to attention. "Any estimates?"

"I think maybe eight friends," Zach said.

"What made you think of eight?" I asked.

"'Cause 40 is a lot of fries!" he replied.

"Maybe seven," said Susan.

After several other students had

shared their estimate, I asked my second question. "How would you go about solving a problem like this?"

"Divide 1,000 by 40, because there's 1,000 fries and 40 in each serving," Pat explained.

"I'd add 40 until I got to 1,000," suggested Susan.

"You could subtract 40 starting with 1,000 until you get to zero," said Sagan.

Jellian used her number sense, starting with a calculation she knew. "I know that 40 times five is 200, so that's five friends right there, so I think it's a lot more than seven or eight," she said, referring to Susan's and Zach's estimates.

"What would you do next?" I asked her.

"Well, I know five friends could eat 200, so I'd figure how many 200s in 1,000," she explained.

I finished reading the book as math period ended. I decided to continue our investigation of 1,000 on the following day.

A Class Discussion

"Yesterday I read you a story in which the author investigated a number of different things," I began. "First, she thought of something she was interested in, like french fries. Then she asked a question that had to do with 1,000 french fries. Do you remember when we thought about how many friends 1,000 french fries would feed?" Students nodded and smiled. "We'll call this a 1,000 question," I told them. "After the

author of the book posed her 1,000 question, she reported the answer."

I then reviewed the book, reminding the children of the things that had been discussed: stars, dandelions, acorns, oak trees, books, hockey, french fries, money, running, etc. I then asked them what things they were interested in and filled half of the chalkboard with their ideas: basketball, science, math, social studies, art, Europe, animals, dinosaurs, Goosebumps books, reptiles, cheetahs. The list was a long one.

When I finished writing all of their ideas on the chalkboard, I modeled a 1,000 question about something I was interested in. "I'm about to read a book called *The Spanish Civil War,* I told the class. "It's 1,000 pages long, and I'm wondering about how long it will take me to read it." I wrote the question on the chalkboard: *How long will it take to read 1,000 pages in the book The Spanish Civil War?* "Now I want you to think of something you're interested in and ask a 1,000 question about it. Raise your hand when you have an idea." I waited till most hands were raised, then called on Christopher.

"How many Animorphs books would 1,000 pages be?" he said.

"Did people know about technology 1,000 years ago?" was Susan's question.

Sagan suggested, "How loud would it sound if 1,000 dogs were barking?"

Kay wanted to know, "About how many bottles of juice would it take to feed 1,000 parakeets at the Wild Animal Park?"

"Now that we have a few examples of 1,000 questions, I'd like to take one topic and develop a number of 1,000 questions around it," I said. I wrote *The Boxcar Children* on the chalkboard. "Everyone please think of a 1,000 question about this series of books, which I know most of you like. I'll write your questions on the chalkboard."

"How long would it take to read 1,000 pages?" was Mike's suggestion.

"How many books could you buy with $1,000?" added Alexa.

"How much would 1,000 of those books weigh?" was what Reba wondered.

Joe raised his hand: "How many Boxcar Children books would you read if you read 1,000 pages?"

A Writing Assignment

"These are interesting examples of different questions you could ask about this topic," I told the class. "I'm going to give each of you a piece of paper, and I'd like you to write your name, a topic you're interested in, and several 1,000 questions that you could investigate."

One aspect of assessment involves gathering information about what students know and what they don't know, what their misconceptions are and what they understand. Listening to students' conversations informs my teaching and guides my instruction. As I walked around the classroom while the children worked, I found that some

of them had a good grasp of 1,000 and others didn't.

Khoa was interested in the length of 1,000 dinosaurs and was busy determining the length of one. Joe wanted to find out how many thousands of miles it is from the United States to Europe. Susan wanted to know if people knew about technology 1,000 years ago. Figure 8.1 shows Pat's baseball questions. I overheard Mike wonder aloud whether 1,000 solar systems would fit in the world. Someone at his table said that was impossible, because we're part of the solar system! I wondered what Mike thought of when he imagined the size of a solar system and if he really knew what one was.

After about twenty minutes, I called the students to attention and gave them further directions. "I'm going to give you a new piece of paper, and I'd like each of you to choose one of your 1,000 questions and recopy it. Then I'd like you to make an illustration and estimate the answer to your question. Remember, when you write down your estimate, include an explanation about your reasoning."

Observing the Students

The children's questions and estimates were interesting and revealed much about their understanding of 1,000 and the multiples of 1,000. I walked from table to table asking questions, listening to conversations, and helping when I was needed.

Case was interested in Legos and wondered how much 1,000 big Lego

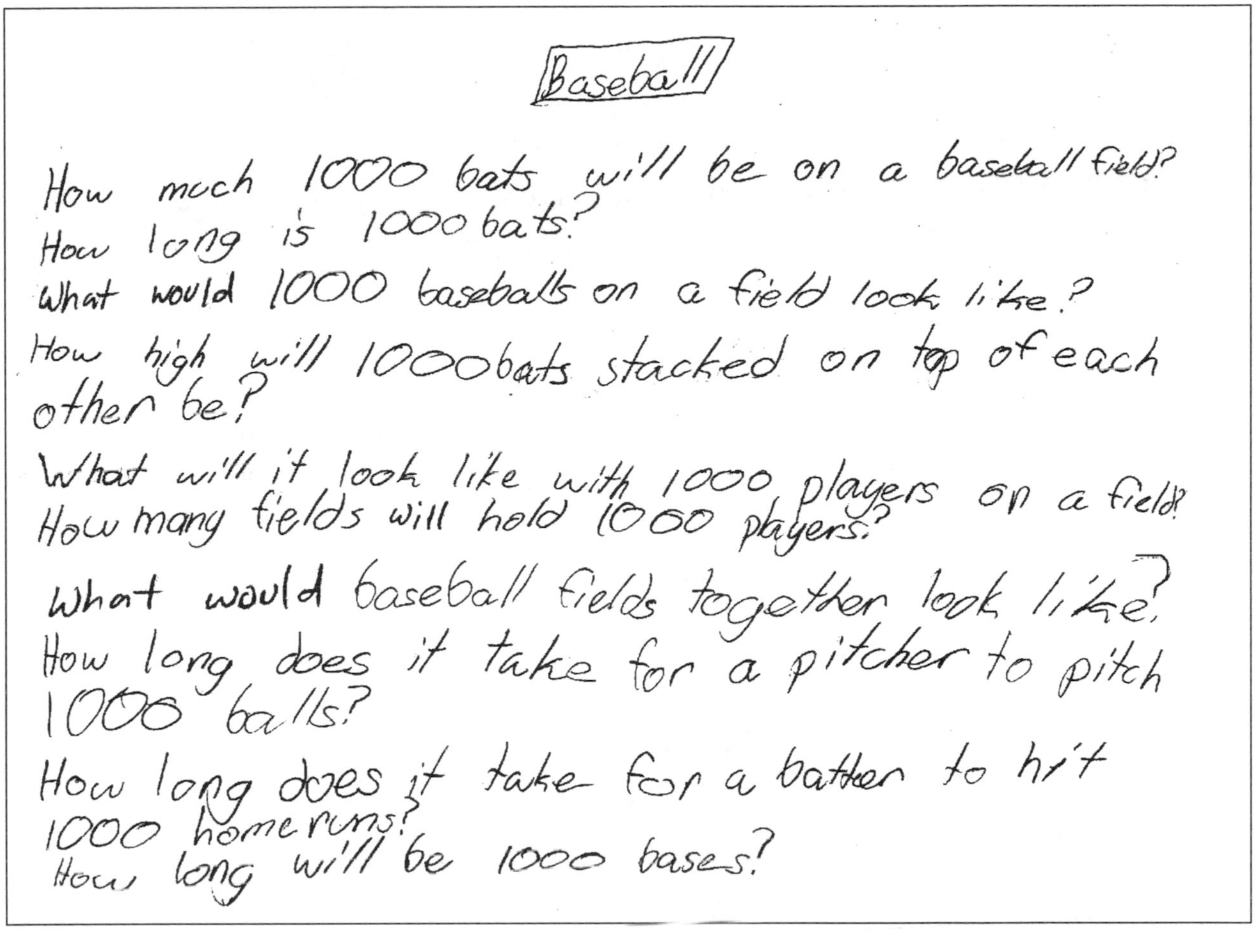

Baseball!

How much 1000 bats will be on a baseball field?
How long is 1000 bats?
What would 1000 baseballs on a field look like?
How high will 1000 bats stacked on top of each other be?
What will it look like with 1000 players on a field?
How many fields will hold 1000 players?
What would baseball fields together look like?
How long does it take for a pitcher to pitch 1000 balls?
How long does it take for a batter to hit 1000 home runs?
How long will be 1000 bases?

FIGURE 8.1
Pat brainstormed "1,000" questions about baseball.

sets would cost. His estimate: *I think it would cost 1,000,000 $ because 1 big set cost like 50 $. I know because my parents bought me one big set* (see figure 8.2). Assessing a student's understanding often generates more questions than answers. I wondered whether Case would realize how far off his estimate was once he figured the correct answer. Would he have a sense of the difference between $50,000 (the correct answer) and $1,000,000?

Sagan likes dogs and wondered whether there could be 1,000 spots on a dalmatian. Her estimate: *Maybe because there's about 50 spots on a puppy that's just getting its spots and when it grows it gets older it gets lots more spots.*

AnaMaria, like Sagan, used a benchmark to help her make an estimate. Her question: *What would 1,000 bugs look like stacked up?* Her estimate: *I estimate about ten meters because about 100 bugs to one meter.* She drew a picture of a child holding a meter stick with 100 bugs on it. Using

How much will 1000 big lego set cost?!

Estiment: I think it would cost 1000,000 $ beccaues I big set cost like 50$ I know because My perents bought me one big set.

Jiny check
to: Toys R US
Pay: 1,000,000 $
from: Case

FIGURE 8.2

Case's estimated answer to his question was unreasonable.

appropriate benchmarks when estimating is useful and is an indicator of number sense.

Eric wondered how long 1,000 basketballs placed one next to the other would be. When I approached him, he was busy drawing 1,000 little basketballs on his paper, but he was stuck on coming up with an estimate. I asked him a question to stimulate his thinking. "Eric, do you know how wide a basketball is?"

Eric had his basketball nestled between his knees. He looked at it,

then looked up at me. "I'd say about a foot wide," he said.

"About how long do you think 1,000 basketballs would be?" I then asked.

"About 1,000 feet!" he exclaimed.

Pat wondered how long it takes for a pitcher to pitch 1,000 balls. His estimate: *I think it would take 1 season to pitch 1000 balls. I used a calculator. I estimated a pitcher pitches 50 pitches per game and plays 20 games a year. I got 1000. The math problem was 50 × 20 = 1000 (see figure 8.3). It's clear*

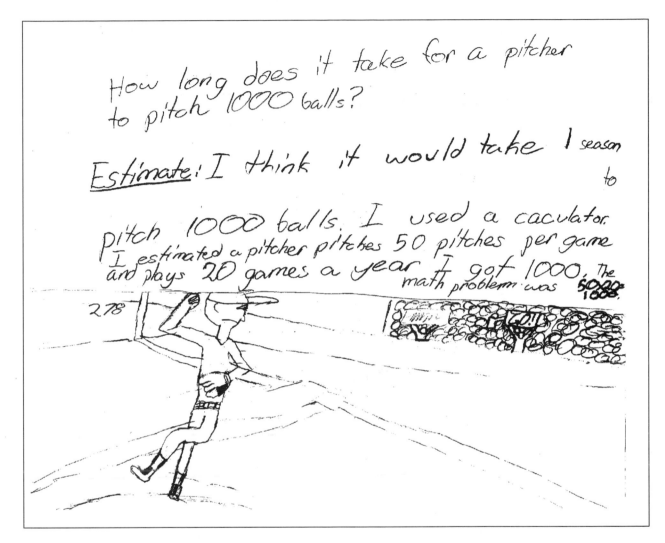

How long does it take for a pitcher to pitch 1000 balls?

Estimate: I think it would take 1 season to pitch 1000 balls. I used a caculator. I estimated a pitcher pitches 50 pitches per game and plays 20 games a year I got 1000. The math problem was 50x20= 1000.

278

FIGURE 8.3

Pat's estimated answer to one of his baseball questions.

from Pat's explanation that he has a good feel for numbers and estimation. Knowing a lot about baseball also helped him know that 50 pitches per game and 20 games per year are reasonable numbers to use.

Students asked questions about height, area, length, width, time, weight, distance, and amounts of money. Alexa wondered how many 50-pound bags of dog food would be needed to feed 1,000 dogs in one day! Asha was interested in finding out how much space 1,000 polar bears would take up. And Christopher wanted to know how long it would take to read 1,000 Animorphs books. His estimate: *I think it will take me six months because they have about 155 pages. It takes me three days to read one* (see figure 8.4).

FIGURE 8.4

Christopher's question and estimated answer.

Continuing the Activity

The next day I wanted the students to investigate their 1,000 question. I gathered the class on the rug and explained the task. "Today you're going to figure out the answer to your 1,000 question and see how the answer compares with your estimate," I began. "You'll need to reread your question, look at your estimate, and think about what you need to do in order to find an answer." Most students nodded their head, indicating that they understood what they were supposed to do.

However, some students looked unsure so I decided to offer an example. "Remember our Boxcar Children example?" I asked. Everyone did. "One of the questions we asked was how many Boxcar Children books would you read if you read 1,000 pages. How might we figure out the answer to this question? Talk with someone next to you about how you could solve it." After a moment, I asked for their attention and repeated the question. At first only a few hands popped up, but as I waited, many more students raised their hand. I called on Susan.

"You'd have to know how many pages are in one Boxcar Children book," she said.

"There's about 100," Alexa volunteered.

"Okay, you'd divide 1,000 by 100 to get your answer," Susan continued.

"Or you could add 100 till you get to 1,000," added Christopher.

"So first you have to figure out what information is needed, like how many pages there are in one book," I said. "Then you might have to do some arithmetic to find the answer. Any questions?"

"So what's the answer?" asked Rick. Several hands shot up. I called on Pat.

"I remember from the other day that there's ten 100s in 1,000, so about 10 books would take up 1,000 pages," reasoned Pat. His ability to apply what he knew about 1,000 to this new problem was further evidence of his well-developed sense of numbers.

The more I worked with Maryann's class and the more questions I posed, the more information I was able to gather about their number sense. It is this experience with children over time that allows a teacher to build a profile of students' understanding about numbers.

"What you're to do is figure out the answer to your 1,000 question and explain how you got your answer using words and numbers," I instructed. I passed back their papers, which I had

collected at the end of math period the day before, and students returned to their seats to investigate their question.

Observing the Students

While some students searched for encyclopedias and calculators and got right to work, others raised their hand immediately. I reminded them that they could solicit help from students at their table.

Some of the questions students were investigating were not easy to answer. Rick wondered what would happen if 1,000 dinosaurs stomped the whole state of California. He predicted that it would create an earthquake! We both agreed that measuring the effect of 1,000 dinosaur stomps would be impossible, given that dinosaurs are extinct. I suggested that he think of another question that could be more easily investigated.

Mike wondered whether 1,000 people liked Alan Iverson, an NBA basketball player for the Philadelphia '76ers. His prediction: *Yes, because 3 people I know like him. Imagine the rest!* I suggested that he collect data about his question in order to verify his prediction. Instead of collecting data, he made a conjecture that included some logic: *I still think the same because a lot of people like him in Philadelphia and that's where the home team is so I think 1,000 people will like him!*

However, most students were able to use mathematics to answer their 1,000 questions. Christopher wondered how long it would take him to read 1,000 Animorphs books. He'd estimated that it would take six months. When investigating the answer, Christopher wrote: *3 × 1,000. I'm counting by threes because it takes me three days to read one book. I have to read 1,000 books. I counted by 3s: 3, 6, 9, 12, 15, 18, 21. I realized I can just add 1,000 3 times. So it would probably take me 3000 days to read 1,000 Animorphs books. 3000 days is about $7^1/_2$ years and some left over days. I figured out $7^1/_2$ years by $2^1/_2$ years which is about 1,000 days. Six months was my estimate. I was way off. I was 7 years off.*

Sagan had estimated that there could be 1,000 spots on a dalmatian, because a puppy has about 50 spots. Her investigation led her to an encyclopedia. She wrote: *There's about 240 spots on a full grown dalmatian. I used a picture in an encyclopedia. There was about 120 on one side then I doubled it for the other side. I got 240. It would take 5 dalmatians to make 1,000 spots.*

In Joe's initial estimate of the distance from the United States to Europe, he thought that if you traveled 1,000 miles, you would circle the globe five times. Using a map, Joe discovered that 1,000 miles isn't as far as he originally thought. He wrote: *I am doing San Diego to Germany. It's only 1,000 miles from San Diego to Oklahoma. It's 6,000 miles from San Diego to Germany. I estimated too far.*

Susan, investigating whether people knew about technology 1,000 years ago, consulted an encyclopedia and wrote: *Technology refers to all the ways people use their inventions. Cars, computers, fax machines, airplanes, and submarines are all examples of technology. 200 years ago was the beginning of power driven machines. Before that, people could still build houses, pyramids, and cities.*

On the second day of the investigation, Case had estimated that 1,000 Lego sets at 50 dollars each would cost a million dollars. Researching his question, he realized his error through simple arithmetic. He wrote: *Each big pack costs at least $50. I used a calculator. I put 50 × 1,000 and it = 50,000. Then I checked it by adding 1,000 50 times. My estimate was $950,000 off. I figured that out by using a calculator. I pushed in 1,000,000 and subtracted 50,000 and it = 950,000. I could of bought 19,000 more sets. I know that because I pushed in 950,000 divided by 50 and it = 19,000.*

Case's written description revealed the sophistication of his reasoning. Initially I had questioned Case's number sense and wondered what his reaction would be to the difference between his estimate and the actual answer. Knowing what students understand and don't understand is difficult. A teacher needs to listen as students work together, pay attention to their responses in class discussions, and assign written work that can provide further insights into how they reason.

RUSTY ANSWERS YOUR QUESTIONS

What is the purpose of this activity?

This activity, based on a children's story, helps students build number sense in several ways. The story suggests many different ways to think about and visualize the number 1,000. Students further develop the concept of 1,000 by posing questions and creating their own contexts for exploring the number. Because our number system is based on the powers of ten, 1,000 and other multiples of ten are important numbers for students to know about.

Understanding what numbers mean as quantities, in context, and in relation to other numbers are all important aspects of number sense. In fact, one cannot make sense of numbers without attaching meaning to them. Manipulating numbers without having a sense of their quantity is like decoding words without under-standing what they mean.

Why did you have students estimate before finding the answer to their 1,000 question?

Having the students estimate an answer to their 1,000 question let me assess whether they have a sense of the effect operations have on numbers. For example, Case wondered how much 1,000 big Lego sets would cost if each set cost $50. His estimate of a million dollars allowed me to tap into his sense of how big or how small the answer might be. When Case calculated the exact answer, he was able to compare it with his estimate, giving him valuable feedback and an opportunity to compare quantities.

Having students estimate first gives them a stake in the results: they want to find out whether their

estimates were reasonable. Children need to have opportunities to think about the reasonableness of estimates in the context of real-life situations like the ones in this activity.

Can I use this activity in third grade?

We often expect children to understand and work with numbers that are beyond their reach. Even adults find references to things like "trillion-dollar budgets" or "billion-dollar debts" very difficult to comprehend. Students can often read and write very large numbers, but understanding these numbers and the quantities they represent is a very different thing.

In third grade, some students may be able to understand what the number 1,000 means; for others, it will be too large. In every class there's a range of understanding and ability. The number 100 might be more appropriate for some third graders. You shouldn't expect all third graders to be able to work with the number 1,000.

Nevertheless, this activity can be adjusted for different grade levels and for different students within a class. While some students work on the number 1,000, others can explore 100, 10,000, or even 1,000,000.

What's the benefit of having students generate their own problems to solve?

Putting children in charge of making sense of a problem gives them the opportunity to develop their number sense. The problems that students create and solve in this activity push them to apply the concepts and skills they've learned in new and different ways. They develop a 1,000 question, define the problem to be solved, identify the numbers and operations to be used, and perform the calculations in a way that makes sense to them. For example, Christopher wonders how long it will take him to read 1,000 Animorphs books and then needs to figure out a way to answer his question. First he thinks about how long it takes him to read one book (three days). This gives him the numbers to use: three and 1,000. Then he starts skip counting by threes until he realizes that he can multiply three times 1,000. This is very different from being given a problem and being told which numbers and operations to use.

9

Stand Up and Be Counted

Overview

Students' number sense is enhanced when they have many opportunities to think about numbers in a variety of ways. At the beginning of this activity, the class brainstorms how to describe the number 25 in as many ways as possible. Then, each student draws a number (1 through 100) at random from a paper bag and, using these earlier ideas as a model, writes sentences that describe this number. Volunteers then take turns reading statements about their number. Students stand up if a statement is also true about their number.

Materials Needed

A 1–100 chart, cut into separate numbers.
A bag or other container.

Teaching Directions

1. Ask students to describe the number 25 in as many ways as they can, and record their ideas on the chalkboard or on a projected transparency.

2. Pass around a bag filled with 100 squares of paper numbered 1 through 100. After each student has drawn a number, ask the class to write down statements that describe their number, just as they did as a class for the number 25.

3. Ask a volunteer to read one statement at a time from his or her list as the other students listen. If a statement is also true about their number, students must

stand up. If a statement isn't true about their number, they must remain seated. (Students who are standing when a statement is read that isn't true about their number must sit down.)

Extension: Same and Different

Have the students, in pairs, compare how their numbers are the same and how they are different.

IN THE CLASSROOM WITH RUSTY

Introducing the Activity

"Today we're going to think about numbers in different ways so that we can see how they're related," I told Pam Long's sixth graders. "Let's start with the number 25." I wrote *25* on the chalkboard. "What comes to your mind when I say 25?"

"It's an odd number," said Michael. I wrote *odd number* on the chalkboard underneath *25.* "What else?" I asked.

"It's a date on the calendar," said Terry. I recorded Terry's comment. (I continued in this vein, adding each new contribution as it was made.)

"It's a square number," offered Rebecca.

"How do you know that?" I asked.

"Because five times five is 25," she said.

"That's true," I confirmed. "Can you explain why 25 is called a square number?"

"Well, because you can make a square that's five inches by five inches," Rebecca explained.

I took a ruler and traced a five-inch-by-five-inch square on the chalkboard. "Like this?" I asked. Rebecca nodded her head in agreement. "Where does the 25 come in?" I inquired.

"Inside the square the area is 25 square inches," she replied.

"Can you show us what you mean on the chalkboard?" I asked her.

Rebecca walked to the front of the room and quickly sketched five rows and five columns, making 25 little squares inside the larger square. Together, we counted the squares by fives. "See, it's shape is a square," said Rebecca. "You could make nine like that too. It would be a three-by-three-inch square."

An important key to developing number sense is asking students to explain their thinking at all times, not just when they make mistakes. Questioning students gives several important messages: you value their ideas; math is about reasoning, not just memorizing; and students should always look to make sense of mathematical problems.

"Other ideas about the number 25?" I continued.

"It's half of 50," said Mindy.

"And it's a quarter of a dollar!" Jenny exclaimed.

"It's the number of pennies in a quarter," added Brennan.

"How could you write that using decimals?" I asked.

"Can I show?" asked Brennan.

"Sure," I replied. Brennan walked up to the board and wrote *.25* next to the sentence he had contributed.

"What else can we say about 25?" I asked.

"It's a multiple of five because you can divide five into 25 evenly," explained Anne.

"You can get to it by counting by fives," said Michael. "That's kind of the same thing that Anne just said."

"It's like two dimes and a nickel," reported Devin.

The ability to represent numbers in a variety of ways is important to number sense. I continued probing. "How else could you make 25?"

"Twenty-four and one more," said Terry.

"One dime and three nickels," added Kimberly.

"It's the answer to 100 divided by four," said Denny.

"It's the date that Christmas falls on!" cried Carl. Everybody laughed.

"Or the weight of a turkey on Thanksgiving!" Ashley exclaimed. The students laughed again.

"How about the cost of a daily newspaper?" said Brennan. "That's how much the *North County Times* costs.

"The ones digit is greater than the tens digit," said Jenny.

I had nearly filled up the chalkboard with their ideas about the number 25. "I have room for one more idea," I said.

"It's a quarter of a century," said Jenny.

At this point I thought the children had enough experience thinking about the number 25, and turned their attention to the brown paper bag I was holding. Before class, I'd cut up a 1–100 chart and placed the little numbered paper squares inside the bag. As I shook the bag, I told the students what was inside.

"As I walk by, I'd like each of you to take one number from the bag," I instructed. "When you get your number, you're to think about it and write down as many statements as you can, just like we did with the number 25. After you've written your statements, we're going to play a game called Stand Up and Be Counted. I'll tell you how to play it when you're finished writing."

After I'd distributed the numbers, I reminded students about what they were to do and gave them about twenty minutes to write. While they worked, I circulated through the room, observing and offering my help when it was needed. (Figures 9.1 and 9.2 are examples of clues two students came up with.) When the twenty minutes were up I called the class back to attention.

"To play Stand Up and Be Counted, a volunteer reads the statements about his or her number, one at a time," I began. "If the statement that's read fits your number, you're going to stand up. If the next statement that's read doesn't fit your number, you sit down. You're to listen to each statement that's read to see whether it's true about your number. We'll practice first using our statements from the number 25 so you can see how the game is played." I read from the board, *"The ones digit is greater than the tens digit."* A few students hesitantly stood up next to their desk. "Remember, if your number's ones digit is greater than the tens digit, please stand up," I reminded them. Several more students stood up. "What numbers might be standing up right now?" I asked.

"Any number like 89 or 34 or 12," said Jenny.

"I think that half the class should be standing," Carl conjectured. "But we didn't use all the numbers in the bag and we don't know which of the numbers between one and 100 people have."

"Why do you think the ones digit

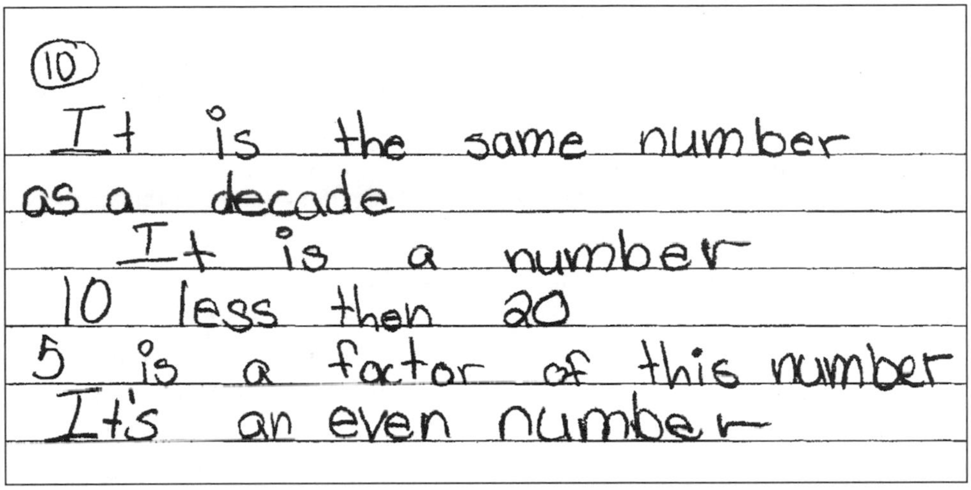

> (10)
> It is the same number as a decade
> It is a number 10 less then 20
> 5 is a factor of this number
> It's an even number

FIGURE 9.1

Michael's clues for the number 10.

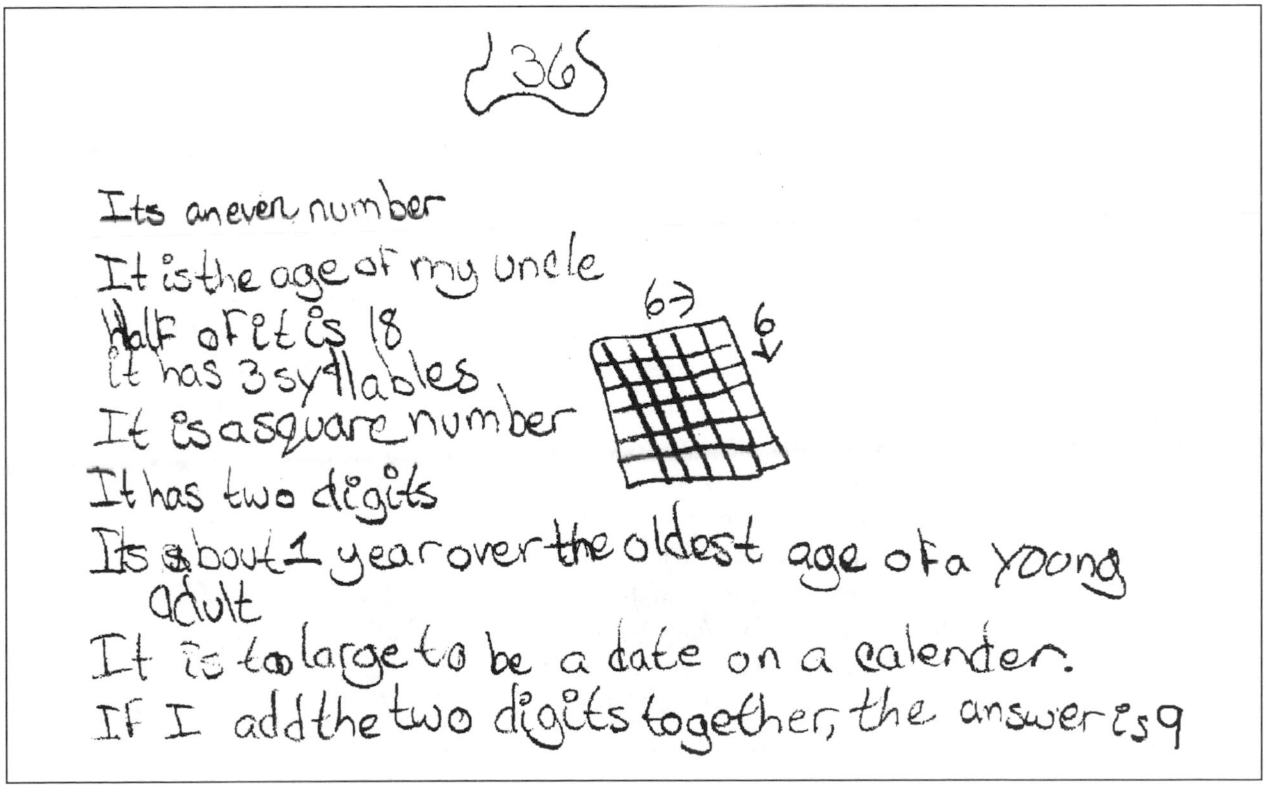

(36)

> Its an even number
> It is the age of my uncle
> Half of it is 18
> It has 3 syllables
> It is a square number
> It has two digits
> Its about 1 year over the oldest age of a young adult
> It is too large to be a date on a calender.
> If I add the two digits together, the answer is 9

FIGURE 9.2

Ashley's clues for the number 36.

is greater than the tens digit in half the numbers between one and 100?" I asked.

"I don't know," Carl began. "It seems like if you've got the digits zero through nine to work with, then about half the time the bigger digit will be in the ones place and about half the time the bigger number will be in the tens place."

"If we colored in a one-to-100 chart, I bet we could count and see," suggested Anne.

"That would be one way to check Carl's idea," I said. "Now I'm going to read the next statement. If you're standing right now, and the next statement fits your number, stay standing. If it doesn't fit your number, please sit down. If you're seated and the statement fits your number, stand up."

"It's an odd number," I read. About half the students stood up.

"It's about half the class again," said Carl. "I think half the numbers are odd and half are even."

I was impressed with Carl's curiosity about numbers. "Are you sure?" I asked. This caused a stir. Although we didn't have time to investigate Carl's conjecture then, I wanted to acknowledge it. "This would be a good question for us to investigate sometime." Then I returned to reading statements from the chalkboard. *"It's a multiple of five."* Several students remained standing, and a few others stood up. "What numbers might be standing up right now?" I asked.

"I think the numbers that are standing up now all either end in zero or five," guessed Michael.

"Why do you think that?" I probed.

"Because if you count by fives, all the multiples either end in zero or five," he explained.

"Count by fives and I'll write the numbers on the chalkboard to see if you're correct," I said to Michael.

"Five, 10, 15, 20, 25, 30 . . . ," he counted while I wrote the numbers. "See, they all end in zero or five." Number sense requires an attitude of sense making on the part of the learner. Michael's confidence with numbers and his ability and determination to identify patterns and see relationships are indicators of number sense.

Next I read, *"One hundred divided by four."* Only Nick remained standing; he had the number 25. "Some statements will be true for many numbers, some for only a few, and some for only one number," I said. "Who would like to read your statements one at a time for the class?" Lots of hands raised. I called on Jenny.

"My number is odd," she began. About half the students stood up. *"My number's digits added together come to five,"* she read. This time, only a few students were standing.

"Which numbers might be standing now?" I asked.

"Numbers like 32, 23, and 41," said Elise.

"Or 50," added Julie.

"My number is a prime number," Jenny continued.

"Can someone describe what a prime number is?" I asked.

"It's a number that has only two factors, like two is prime and it has itself and one as factors and that's all," Don explained.

"What else can we say about prime numbers?" I probed.

"Well, I think most of them are odd but two is prime so not all of them are odd numbers," said Mark.

"I want the students who are standing to call out your number one at a time, and I'll record them on the chalkboard," I said. Students called out 2, 7, 11, 19, 23, and 47. "Let's examine these numbers to see whether they have only one and themselves as factors," I told them. The students studied the numbers, and after a moment most were nodding their head in agreement.

"All of them are odd except for the number two," Mark observed.

"That's correct," I said. I then motioned to Jenny to continue.

"My number is under 40," Jenny read as she finished her statements.

"Okay, Jenny. Tell us what your number is," I said.

"It's 23," she told the class.

"Who else would like to read their statements?" I asked. I called on José.

"My number is even," he began. About half the class stood up. *"My number has two digits."*

"Do I need to have a number that's both even and two digits to stand up?" asked Kimberly.

"Those students with two-digit numbers, even or odd, can stand up now," I replied. "Listen to each clue separately to see whether it's true for your number."

"The sum of my digits is four," José read. Some students sat down, while others stood up.

"What numbers could be standing now?" I asked.

"Thirty-one," said Julie.

"It could also be 22," added Denny.

"Eleven is a factor of my number," José continued.

"What numbers could be standing now?" I asked.

"Forty-four," Katie replied, "because 11 times four is 44."

"Also 22, because 11 times two is 22," Kimberly noted.

"It could be 11, 22, 33, 44, 55, 66, 77, 88, and 99," said Carl. "There's a pattern, too! It's like 11 times one, 11 times two, 11 times 3, like that."

"My number is the number of Emitt Smith of the Cowboys," said José. He then stood up and announced that his number was 22.

"Now let's have students read a statement from their paper that has only one correct answer," I instructed.

Xavier began waving his hand back and forth with enthusiasm. *"The number on Steve Young's jersey!"* he exclaimed. Everyone laughed.

"For those of us who aren't '49er fans or who don't watch football, could you tell us your number?" I asked him.

"My number is eight," he said as he stood up.

"Two times a decade plus ten," said Terry. Xavier sat down and Terry was the only student who stood up.

"My number is the sum of 12 plus 12 and the product of 12 times two," said Devin. Devin stood up and Terry sat down.

"Can someone read a statement so

that more than one person will be standing?" I asked.

"The difference between the digits in my number is one," Anne read.

"What numbers could be standing now?" I asked.

"Numbers like 45 or 54," said Daniel.

"Or numbers like 98 or 89," added Elise.

"My number is a composite number," Katie read.

"What's a composite number?" I asked, suspecting that some students would need clarification.

"It's not a prime number," she answered, "and it has more than two factors." This time, lots of students stood up.

Elise read next. *"It's a number when you are old."* It took a few seconds for students to stand up; many of them were thinking hard about this statement.

"What numbers could be standing up now?" I asked.

"Well, I think it depends on what you think old is," said Andy.

"I'm curious about the numbers that are standing up now," I said.

"My number is 79," said Xavier. "That's how old I think my great-grandmother is, and she's old."

"My number is 45," added Daniel. "That's the age of my dad."

"I wonder what age would be considered old by a kindergartner?" I asked the class.

"Probably 11 or 12, like us!" Jennifer exclaimed. Everyone laughed.

"I agree," I said. "You all would probably seem pretty old to a child who is only five years old. Sometimes

numbers have different meanings depending on the person who is thinking about the numbers." Understanding the relative size or magnitude of numbers is an important element of number sense.

That ended math class for the day, but Pam Long used Stand Up and Be Counted throughout the week as a warm-up. She found that with practice, the game's procedural elements became easier for the students. This freed them to focus on the characteristics of the numbers used and how the numbers were related.

Extending the Activity

Patti Reynolds's fifth graders had been playing Stand Up and Be Counted for several days when I introduced an extension of the activity called Same and Different. I wanted them to focus on how numbers relate to one another. While these fifth graders were building on the work they did with Stand Up and Be Counted, it isn't necessarily a prerequisite.

Each student had already drawn a number from 1 through 100 and had written several statements about this number. Their statements were in front of them on their desks. I began by writing the number 25 at the top of the chalkboard. "Would anyone like to volunteer their number so that I can write it down next to 25?" I asked. Jaime wiggled his hand in the air, desperate to volunteer. I finally called on him.

"Seventy-one," he said. "I don't

like my number. It's too hard to think of things to say about it."

I wrote *71* next to *25* on the chalkboard and asked Jaime why he thought his number was difficult.

"I don't know," he replied. After a few seconds, he said "Maybe because it's a prime number. It's kind of weird."

"Let's see if we can learn more about Jaime's number," I said to the class. "We're going to compare the numbers 25 and 71. I want you to think about how these numbers are the same and how they're different."

"They're both odd numbers," Jaime said. "I knew that already about my number." I wrote *odd numbers* on the chalkboard in the Same column. (I added each successive comment to the chart as the students shared their ideas.)

"They both have two digits," offered Anna.

"Both numbers have themselves as factors," added Joe.

"Seventy-one is prime and 25 is a square number," said Mary. "When we learned how to play Stand Up and Be Counted, we talked about the number 25."

Lots of hands were raised now. I called on Asha.

"Seventy-one is greater than 25," she said.

"The sum of the digits in 25 is seven, and the sum of the digits in 71 is eight," added Vicky.

"When you double 71, you get an answer in the hundreds," said José. "Twenty-five is a landmark number and 71 isn't."

"Explain what you mean by a landmark number, José," I said.

"Well, it's like a number that's easy to work with," he replied. "Like if you have to multiply 26 times five, you could go to 25 times five first and that's easier."

"What other numbers are easy to work with?" I prodded.

"Numbers like ten, 50, and 100," Angela said.

"Or 500 or 1,000," added Jaime.

Landmark numbers are numbers which are familiar landing places, which make for simple calculations (as José pointed out), and to which other numbers can be related. Because our number system is based on powers of ten, the numbers 10, 100, and 1,000 are especially important landmarks. Knowing about these landmark numbers, their multiples, and their factors is the basis of good number sense.

"How else do 25 and 71 compare?" I continued.

"Twenty-five is one fourth of 100 and 71 is almost three fourths of 100," observed Vicky.

"Twenty-five is divisible by five and has three factors, and 71 has only two factors," said Steve.

"Twenty-five is a day of the month and 71 can't be," Krissy said.

A Writing Assignment

When the chart on the chalkboard was filled with phrases describing how the numbers 25 and 71 were the same and how they were different, I gave the students directions for their next task. "Now I'd like for you to find a partner," I began. "When you have a partner, raise your hand and I'll give you a piece of paper. You and your partner will write your names at the top and also write your two numbers. Work together to write as many statements as you can about how your two numbers are the same and how they're different, just like we did with the numbers 25 and 71. I would like you to take turns doing the writing, and remember that each of you needs to contribute ideas."

A Class Discussion

After about thirty minutes, I called the class together for a discussion. "What was easy and what was difficult about this task?" I asked.

"It helped that we already wrote about our numbers before," said Shaun, "and it helped that we worked with a partner. It was more fun."

"I liked taking turns writing," offered Antonio, Shaun's partner. "It made it easier."

"Sometimes it's hard to figure out what factors the numbers have in common," said Angela. "We had to find the factors of each of our numbers and that took some time."

"It helped that we worked with 25 and 71 before to give us an idea about how to do the job," Melissa said.

"Would anyone like to share something you think is interesting about your numbers?" I asked.

"Our numbers were 75 and 66," Tabatha reported. "Vicky told me that the longest-living parakeet has lived 75

years! Also, if you round both of our numbers to the nearest hundred, you'd round them to 100."

"Our numbers are 88 and 87," said José. "They're only one number away from each other, and Roald Dahl's book *Esio Trot* has 88 pages. And if you rounded them to the nearest ten, you'd round them to 90."

"Both of our numbers, 88 and 33, have digits that are the same and both have 11 as a factor," said Carryanne. "Eighty-eight is the age of an old adult and 33 is the age of a young adult." (See figure 9.3 for the rest of Carryanne and her partner's work.)

"Our numbers are 78 and 83," Samuel chimed in. "One is odd and one is even, and when we added them together we got 161, and that's odd. When we multiplied them together we got 6,474 and that's even!" (Samuel and his partner's work is shown in figure 9.4.)

When partners had finished sharing ideas about their numbers, Brandy asked a final question: "Why are we doing this activity?"

I paused and several students giggled nervously. "That's a good question," I said. "Whenever I teach a lesson, I need to know why I'm teaching it and how it helps you with math. I think this is a good activity for several reasons. One is that it helps you recognize that numbers can be used in many different ways. It also helps you understand what numbers mean and how they relate to one another. This activity may also help us all think about math in a different way."

"I think this is a good activity

because it gives me an idea of what you know about numbers," added Patti Reynolds, their teacher. "I'm impressed that you know so much about factors, prime and square numbers, odd and even numbers, and how numbers are used in the world." Later, Patti commented that she thought having the students work together and discuss their thinking was a very effective approach.

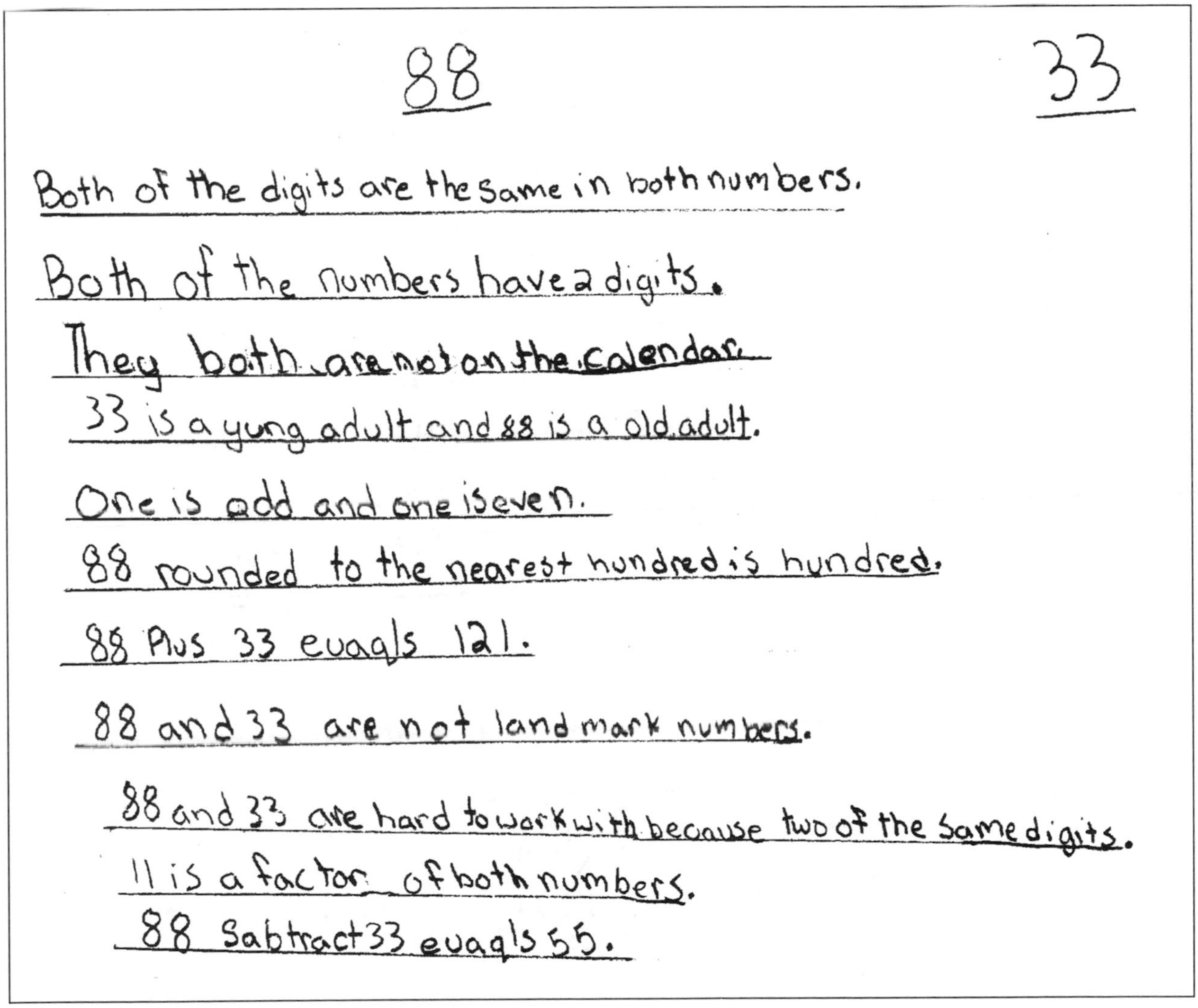

88   33

Both of the digits are the same in both numbers.

Both of the numbers have 2 digits.

They both are not on the calendar.

33 is a yung adult and 88 is a old adult.

One is odd and one is even.

88 rounded to the nearest hundred is hundred.

88 plus 33 evaqls 121.

88 and 33 are not land mark numbers.

88 and 33 are hard to work with because two of the same digits.

11 is a factor of both numbers.

88 sabtract 33 evaqls 55.

FIGURE 9.3

Carryanne and her partner compared 88 and 33.

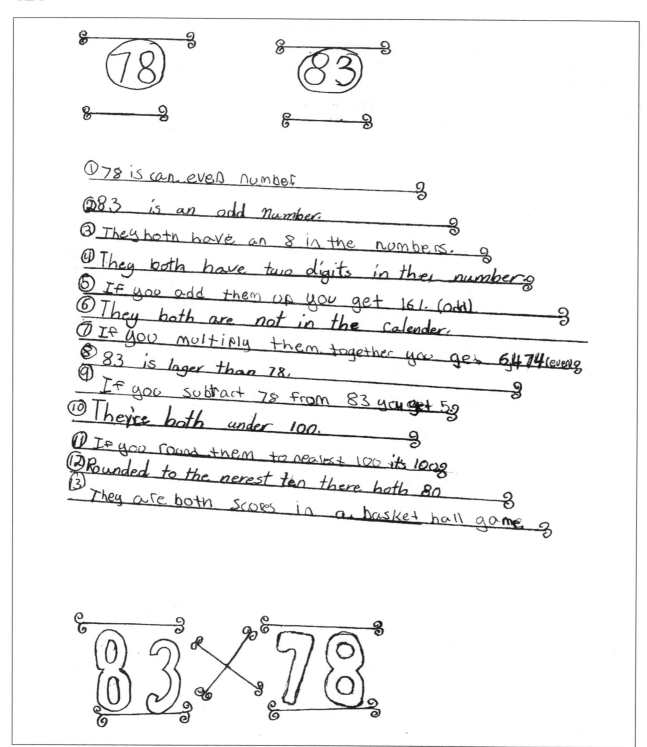

① 78 is can even number.

② 83 is an odd number.

③ They both have an 8 in the numbers.

④ They both have two digits in their numbers.

⑤ If you add them up you get 161. (odd)

⑥ They both are not in the calender.

⑦ If you multiply them together you get 6,474 (even)

⑧ 83 is lager than 78.

⑨ If you subtract 78 from 83 you get 5

⑩ They're both under 100.

⑪ If you round them to nearest 100 its 100

⑫ Rounded to the nerest ten there both 80

⑬ They are both scores in a basket ball game.

FIGURE 9.4

Samuel and his partner compared 83 and 78.

RUSTY ANSWERS YOUR QUESTIONS

What is the purpose of this activity?

Number sense has often been described as good intuition about numbers and their relationships. The purpose of this activity is for students to learn about the characteristics of numbers, to see how they're related, and to use mathematical vocabulary to discuss them.

Are there ways to do the activity differently?

Instead of writing about their numbers individually, students could work with partners. This might provide more support for children who have difficulty thinking about the characteristics of numbers.

There are times during any activity when someone's question or conjecture can lead to a stimulating class discussion. For example, in Pam Long's sixth-grade class, Carl thought that in half of the numbers between one and 100, the digit in the tens place would be larger than in the ones. We didn't have the time to explore this idea fully. It's always a good idea to record on chart paper any ideas about which the class is curious, confused, or in disagreement; that way, it's easier to return to them at a later time.

When doing the Same and Different extension, you might want to talk with students about various ways they can organize their comparisons— a two-column table or a Venn diagram, for example.

What do I do if my students don't have much experience thinking and talking about numbers?

For students with little experience in talking about numbers in different ways, this activity may seem difficult at first. In that case, you may want to model the activity several times before turning the students loose on it themselves. Also, asking the following questions will help students generate ideas:

- How is your number used in the real world?
- Is your number odd or even?
- Is your number prime or composite?
- Is your number a multiple of another number?
- What are the factors of your number?
- What is the sum of the digits in your number?
- In what ways can your number be taken apart and put back together?
- Is your number a square number?
- How many factors does your number have?
- Is it a number of a day of the month?
- Can you relate your number to money? What coins could you use to add up to your number?
- Which is greater, the digit in the ones place or the tens place?
- Does your number have one, two, or three digits?
- Can you relate your number to measurement?

- Can you relate your number to someone's age? Does your number represent the age of a young person? a teenager? an older person?
- What's half of your number? twice your number?
- Can you get to your number counting by twos? fives? tens?
- Is your number greater or less than the number of students in the room?

What are some ways to assess a student's number sense in this activity?

This activity can be used to assess what an individual student or the class as a whole knows about numbers, operations, and mathematical vocabulary. When teaching this activity, keep the following questions in mind:

- Do students know if their number is odd or even?

- Are students familiar with the language of numbers and operations? This might include such things as factor, multiple, sum, difference, divisible, prime numbers, composite numbers, and square numbers.
- Are students able to figure out the factors of their number?
- Do students know whether their number is a multiple of other numbers?
- Do students understand the relative size of numbers? Do they use or understand clues like *more than, less than*, and *halfway between*?
- Are students able to think about numbers in different ways? Can they relate numbers to a variety of contexts?
- Do students understand that numbers can be taken apart and put back together? (For example, the number 50 can be thought of as 25 plus 25, or ten times four plus ten, or 20 plus 20 plus 10, etc.)

10 *Guess My Number*

Overview

Guess My Number is a simple warm-up activity that gets students thinking and participating. Students always enjoy guessing games, and this one gives them practice with thinking about characteristics of numbers as well as experience with thinking strategically. Students guess a secret number from within a range on the basis of being told whether their guesses are greater or less than the number. The game (and variations of it—see the extensions below) can be played many times over the year.

Teaching Directions

1. Choose a secret number.

2. Tell the class the range of numbers your number falls within (1 to 10, 50 to 100, 1 to 100, whatever).

3. Have individual students guess your secret number; if their guess is incorrect, announce whether your number is greater or less than the number guessed.

4. Continue until someone guesses your secret number.

Extensions

1. Choose a secret number within a wider range (1 to 500, 1 to 1000). Then give one clue about your secret number (ends with zero; odd; sum of the digits is ten; etc.). Ask students to investigate the possible numbers and play the game as before.

2. Play the game using a fraction or a decimal as the secret number.

IN THE CLASSROOM WITH CAREN

Introducing the Activity

"I've got a secret number between one and 100," I told Serena Thakur and Dina Calvin's third and fourth graders. "Raise your hand if you want to guess what it is." Almost everyone wanted to guess. I called on Eddie.

"Ten?" he asked.

"My number is greater than ten," I responded.

"How about 50?" suggested Mae.

"My number is greater than 50," I told her.

Since the class was just learning the game, I recorded each child's guess on a projected transparency, and drew an up arrow next to it to indicate my number was greater. (Sometimes I play the game without giving any visual clues. Then the students are forced to listen very carefully to each guess and remember my responses.) I called on Hans next.

"Ninety?" he guessed.

"My number is less than 90," I said as I wrote down *90* and drew a down arrow next to it.

"Sixty-five?" guessed Carolina.

"My number is greater," I replied.

"Fifty-one?" asked Antoine.

"My number is greater than 51," I told him.

Some of the students were less than pleased with Antoine's guess. Since I had already said that my number was greater than 65 and less than 90, most of the students knew my number was somewhere between 66

and 89. Antoine's guess of 51 was superfluous. There were a few snorts and heavy sighs.

Since a safe environment in which to think about new ideas and take risks is critical to a successful math class, I needed to address this head on. I was concerned that Antoine and several other students would be reluctant to participate if the threat of humiliation loomed. As a teacher, I need to provide the appropriate arena and set the proper tone. I can't let snide comments or belittling remarks slide by. I need to show the class, through my words and actions, that all thinking is valued and all individuals are respected.

"When we are learning a new game like this," I told the class, "all guesses are fine. It's not okay to make anyone feel bad about his guess. Everyone has the right to think and talk about his ideas without feeling bad. If people are worried about being made fun of, they're not able to do their best thinking. Brain researchers have proved this. Your brain doesn't work as well when you don't feel safe and respected. So, when someone says something, even if you disagree, you need to listen quietly and respond respectfully. Does everyone understand why this is so important?" I paused, making eye contact with everyone. "Now, who else has a guess?"

"Sixty-nine?" Donald ventured.

"My number is greater than 69," I told him as I recorded it on the overhead.

"Seventy-three?" offered Reggie.

"My number is greater than 73 also," I answered. I pointed to the numbers and arrows on the overhead, which were:

> *90* ↓
> *65* ↑
> *51* ↑
> *69* ↑
> *73* ↑

"Okay, I'm going to give you a minute or two to talk at your tables about my secret number. Tell each other what you think you know about my number and what number you might want to guess next." After a short time, I called everyone back to attention. "Can someone tell us something you think you know about my secret number? I'm not asking for a guess right now. I'm asking *about* my number."

"We know it's less than 90 and greater than 73," Abbie said.

"All right," I replied.

"I think it's in the 80s, most likely," added Jack.

"Why do you think that?" I questioned.

"Because there's more numbers left in the 80s than in the 70s," Jack explained. "It can't be 70 or 71 or 72 or 73 because we already guessed 73 and you said it's greater. But it can be anywhere in the 80s."

Brief discussions like this help build number sense. Having students think, talk, and explain their views helps them build confidence and strengthen their understanding of the number system. Students have time to consider relative quantities and use concepts such as greater than, less than, and in between. They also use

logical thinking to try to narrow down the possibilities.

I asked for another guess.

"Eighty?" asked Hans.

"My number is greater," I told him.

"Eighty-nine?" guessed Carolina.

"It's less than 89. Put a thumb up if you think you have a pretty good idea of what my number might be," I directed the class. I wanted to make sure everyone was still actively involved. "Okay, raise your hand if you want to guess." I called on Mae.

"Eighty-five?"

"My number is greater than 85."

"Eighty-eight?" guessed Eddie.

"Yes. That's my number. Now let's try the super challenging version of Guess My Number," I invited. "This time I'm going to pick a secret number between one and 500. That's a lot of numbers. Since there are so many possibilities I'm going to give you one hint. The hint is that my number ends with a zero. Would someone give us an example of a number that's possible?" Many students were ready and willing.

"One hundred," suggested Andy.

"Yes, 100 is possible because 100 ends with zero," I agreed. "How about an impossible number? Can you give an example of a number you can definitely eliminate?"

"Two hundred and sixty-eight," offered Joaquin.

"Right," I said, "because 268 ends with eight and not zero. So who wants to guess my number?"

"How about 410?" volunteered Linda.

"My number is less." I wrote *410* with a down arrow next to it.

"Three hundred and thirty?" asked Eddie.

"Less," I replied.

Ryan tried 150.

"It's greater than 150," I told him.

Introducing an Investigation

Since the students understood the parameters and were engaged in thinking about the numbers, this seemed like a good time to push a little harder. "I'm getting curious about something. I wonder how many numbers there are between one and 500 that end in zero."

"Fifty," Andy blurted out almost instantly.

I ignored her for the moment. "I'm going to give you a little time to talk at your tables about this. Don't just come up with an answer. I want to hear how you figured it out. Use paper and pencil so you can prove your idea."

Observing the Students

While the students worked on this question, I circulated. I asked Andy about her answer. "It's simple," she explained, "because every ten numbers ends with zero, and 500 divided by ten is 50." It took me a moment to digest this. Andy realized that numbers that end with zero are multiples of ten. So she had divided 500 into groups of ten to find out how many multiples of ten there were. Those numbers would be the numbers that end in zero. I was impressed with her number sense. She clearly had a grasp of the problem and understood how to use division to find the answer.

Although the question itself hadn't been much of a challenge for Andy, I decided to push her by asking her to write about her thinking. "Wow," I said, "that's an interesting way to think about it. Can you write that down and explain it on your paper? That way I'll be able to remember."

Donald also had a "chunking" approach. He counted by tens on his fingers to 100. "Oh, it's 50," he announced upon reaching 100.

"How do you know?" I asked.

He explained. "There's 10 numbers that end in zero up to 100, so times that by five for 500."

I visited some other tables to see how they were doing. My visits uncovered a range of thinking, and I was able to make some important observations about the students' number sense. Carolina was struggling with 50 times ten. She had been sitting next to Andy and had overheard our earlier conversation. I think she was trying to use Andy's idea, which didn't really make sense to her. I asked her why she chose the numbers 50 and 10, and she couldn't tell me. I was also alarmed to see she was implementing the standard multiplication algorithm to solve the problem. She had written:

$$\begin{array}{r} 50 \\ \times\ 10 \\ \hline 00 \\ 50\ \ \\ \hline 500 \end{array}$$

Why did she go to all that trouble? If there was ever a problem for a fourth grader to solve mentally, 50×10 is it. Was it possible that she really didn't have the ability to solve the equation any other way? Or had she just been programmed to deal with all multiplication problems only in this way? Did she stop to think about the numbers at all before she began? I couldn't make a judgment about Carolina's number sense from this one event. I had a lot more to find out about her. I knew she was struggling with the problem in general, so I didn't want to put additional pressure on her at the moment. I needed to get back to her in another context and ask her to solve 50×10 in her head. That way I'd know if she was able to do it mentally and she just didn't think to use mental arithmetic in this situation.

Some other students were counting by tens and writing each number down. Then they were counting up all the numbers on their paper. Others were counting by tens aloud and keeping track with their fingers. While these methods didn't have the elegance of Andy's, the students were at least organizing their work in a systematic way.

I was concerned about the students who were just randomly writing numbers that ended in zero. They didn't seem to be organizing their work or taking control of the problem. Joey, for example, had started by writing the guesses the class had started with: 410, 330, 150. Then he continued adding to the list: 240, 60, 110 . . . .

"So what's your plan?" I asked, trying to hint that a plan is a good thing.

"I'm writing down numbers that end with zero," he replied.

"How will you know you found them all?" I asked, again hinting at a bigger picture.

"I'll just count them when I'm done."

The conversation appeared to be going nowhere. I decided to let him continue his haphazard quest for the moment. I counted on the upcoming whole-class discussion to help him see other ways to think about the job.

Continuing the Activity

It was time we finished the game we had started. I referred to the three clues we already had. "So you know my number is less than 410, less than 330, and more than 150. You also know a lot about numbers that end in zero from all the work you just did. Who would like to take a guess?" I called on Chalisa.

"Two hundred and fifty?" she asked.

"My number is greater."

"Three hundred and fifty?" Reggie tried.

"My number is less."

"Three hundred," guessed Abbie.

"My number is less than 300," I replied.

"It has to be 260, 270, 280, or 290," Donald volunteered.

"Really?" I challenged.

"Yeah," interjected Andy, "because it's between 250 and 300."

"How about 280?" Eddie asked.

"My number is less."

"Two hundred and seventy," Jack stated with authority.

"My number is less," I announced. The students now knew my secret number and hands were flailing frantically. Rather than pick one student to be the hero, I decided to let the whole group answer. "Put your hands down please," I asked as I waited for calm. "I'm going to count to three, and when I say three you will use your indoor voice to say the answer. One. Two. Three."

"Two hundred and sixty!!!" was the enthusiastic chorus in a slightly louder tone than I had bargained for.

"That's right," I acknowledged. "So now you know how to play the super challenging version of Guess My Number. Maybe next time one of you can think of a secret number and a hint and we can try to guess your number." The students seemed excited by the possibility.

Using the Activity with Sixth Graders

I started the activity with Pam Long's sixth graders exactly as I had with the third and fourth graders. We played a quick game with a number between one and 100. Then we moved on to a number between one and 500 that ended in zero, this time going right into a whole-class discussion about how many possibilities there were rather than taking time for each table to work on it first.

Then I started a third game with the class, in which I planned to pose a lengthier investigation. "Okay," I said, "this time I've got a number between one and 500. I have one hint for you. The digits in my number add up to ten. Can anyone give an example of a number it might be?" I called on Courtney.

"Nineteen," she said.

"Yes," I agreed, as I wrote *19* on the board, "19 works because one plus nine equals ten. How about another example?"

"Two hundred and eighty," volunteered Albert.

"Right," I responded, "because two plus eight plus zero equals ten. How about some other possibilities?"

"Four hundred and forty-two," said Mousqa.

"Six hundred and forty." This came from Johnna.

As I wrote *640* on the board, several students protested. At first I didn't understand their concern. "What's wrong with 640?" I asked. "Six and four and zero make ten."

"Yeah," explained Edwin, "but it's supposed to be between one and 500."

"Oh, I see." I turned to Johnna. "You're right that the sum of the digits of 640 equals ten, but 640 is more than 500. So it can't be my secret number."

Introducing an Investigation

Seeing that the students understood my rule, I decided to incorporate a bit of estimation. "So, I have this secret number somewhere between one and 500. You know there are fewer than

500 possibilities, because the number has to have digits that add up to ten. I wonder how many numbers there are between one and 500 that fit my rule. When we played Guess My Number earlier, we found that there are 50 numbers between one and 500 that end with zero. Do you think there are more or fewer numbers with digits that add up to ten? Let's get some estimates."

"I think there are going to be 50 again," speculated Bryan.

"I'd say 100," countered Serena.

"Probably 55," Andy estimated

"More like 400!" Vicky jumped in.

I accepted all the estimates without comment. My goal was to get students to think and make predictions. They really didn't have enough information or experience to make an accurate judgment at this point. I just wanted them to start to think—and wonder—so they'd be motivated to investigate.

"Okay, here's the plan," I proceeded. "You're going to have some time to work at your tables to investigate this question. Just how many numbers are there between one and 500 whose digits add up to ten? You'll probably want to use paper and pencil to organize your work and keep track of the numbers you find. I also think it will be very helpful for you to work together and talk at your tables. There are probably different ways you can work on this problem so you can get a lot of ideas from one another. After you've had some time to investigate we'll get back together to discuss your findings and to play Guess My Number. Are there any questions

about your job right now?" The students were clear on the assignment, so I let them get to work.

Observing the Students

The investigation was very rich, and I had a lot of time to circulate throughout the room while the students worked on the problem. My visits to different tables were fascinating and told me a great deal about the students' number sense. The primary insight I gained was about different views of the number system. Many of the students began randomly listing numbers that fit the rule. Others began systematically, breaking the range of one to 500 into smaller, more manageable groups of 100. As they continued working, quite a few of the students noticed patterns emerging. The patterns were powerful tools for organizing their papers and for establishing the total number of possibilities. I talked to the children while they were working and I also had them write a little about their plan of attack and how they found all the possibilities.

Quite a few tables figured out how to apply the commutative property to identifying numbers that fit the clue. If 19 works, 91 works; if 361 works, so do 163, 136, 316, 613, and 631. As Kate wrote: *Well first we tried to figure out what adds up to ten and we wrote the numbers on a piece of paper and I also got some numbers by putting them backward like: 73–37, 91–19, 64–46.*

Bhavna found a handy use for zero. After she had written all the two-digit possibilities, she added zero to the end of them for a bunch more.

Edwin noticed that if one digit is decreased by a certain amount while another digit is increased by the same amount, the sum stays the same. He used this discovery to help him organize his work. He wrote: *I started by looking for the smallest number that equals 10. I got 19. After that I went on and got 28. Right when I got 28 a pattern popped in my head. Mousqa and I started this pattern. It was to make the tens digit number to go up one and the ones digit number to go down one. 19, 28, 37, 46 . . . . But after you finish the pattern with the tens you look for the lowest number that equals 10 but in the one hundreds, then 2, 3 and 4 hundreds. But you do the exact pattern as you did in the tens.* Edwin had then systematically listed every number using the method he had described: 19, 28, 37, 46, 55, 64, 73, 82, 91,

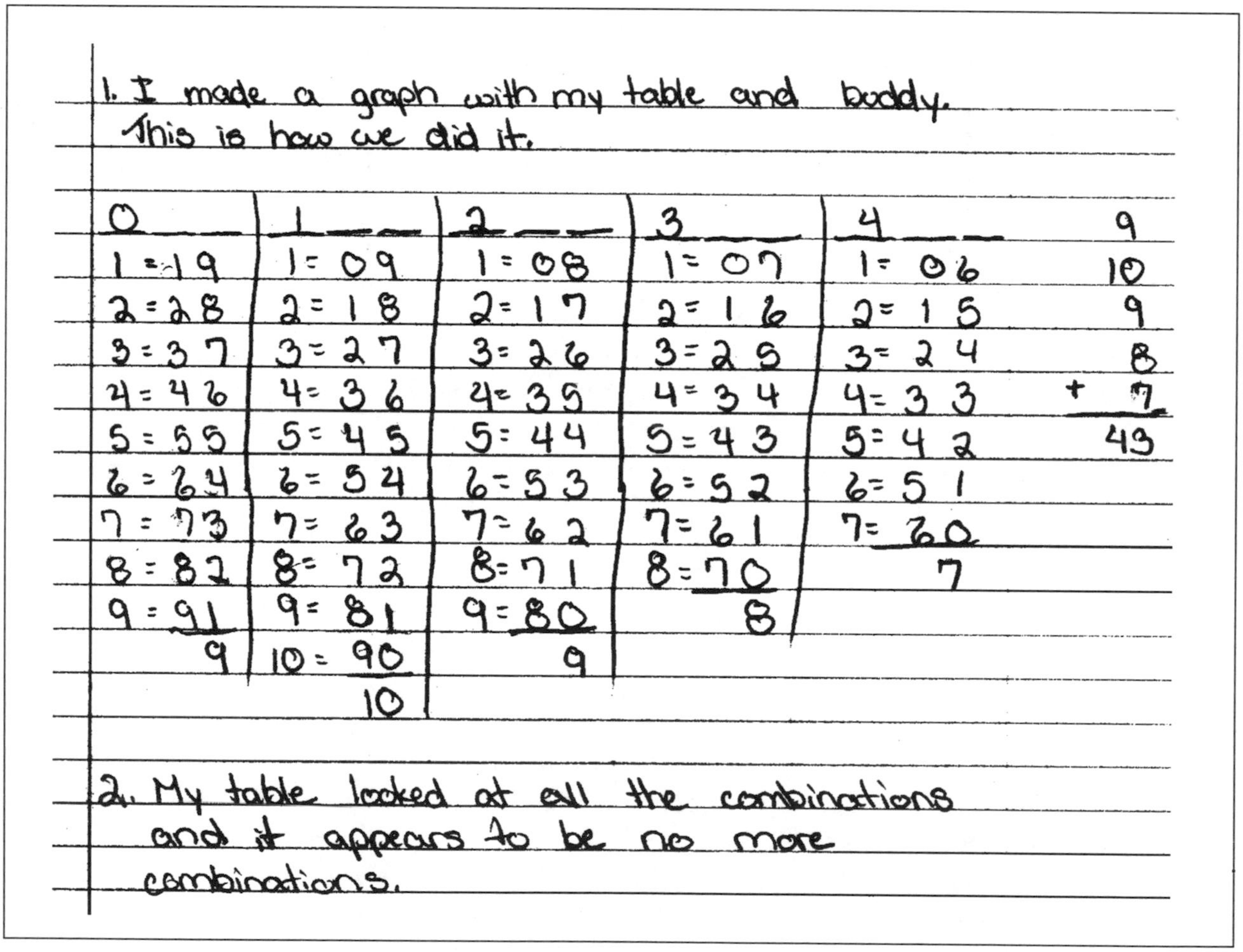

1. I made a graph with my table and buddy. This is how we did it.

0	1	2	3	4	9
1 = 19	1 = 09	1 = 08	1 = 07	1 = 06	10
2 = 28	2 = 18	2 = 17	2 = 16	2 = 15	9
3 = 37	3 = 27	3 = 26	3 = 25	3 = 24	8
4 = 46	4 = 36	4 = 35	4 = 34	4 = 33	+ 7
5 = 55	5 = 45	5 = 44	5 = 43	5 = 42	43
6 = 64	6 = 54	6 = 53	6 = 52	6 = 51	
7 = 73	7 = 63	7 = 62	7 = 61	7 = 60	
8 = 82	8 = 72	8 = 71	8 = 70	7	
9 = 91	9 = 81	9 = 80	8		
9	10 = 90	9			
	10				

2. My table looked at all the combinations and it appears to be no more combinations.

FIGURE 10.1
Albert used columns to organize his work.

109, 118, 127, 136, 145, 154, 163, and so on.

Interestingly, he was not confident that he had found all the numbers. He wrote at the end of his paper: *I don't think you will know all of these numbers through 1 and 500. But if you work on this problem for maybe a while you can find them all.* This taught me a valuable lesson. Even when children find patterns, they need time to realize their usefulness and applicability. The search for and discovery of patterns in the number system is a fundamental building block of number sense. However, the next step is to use these patterns to help solve problems. The connection does not occur automatically. Children need many opportunities to use the patterns in order to appreciate their value in problem solving.

Several tables used columns as their organizing tactic. Some students divided their paper into five categories, 1–100, 100–200, 200–300, 300–400, and 400–500. Then they listed all the possibilities under each column, some doing so randomly, others being more organized.

Albert focused on the digits in each column to provide additional organization. He headed each column with three lines, for three digits. Then he filled in the first digit of each column and listed the possibilities for the second and third digits underneath (see figure 10.1). I was intrigued by the elegance of this method, which reveals several patterns at once. Looking across the rows shows one pattern. Going down each column shows the pattern Edwin described. The total number of

possibilities in each column also appears to have a bell shape and corresponding numerical pattern, 9, 10, 9, 8, 7. I was impressed. Here was an opportunity to consider many properties of numbers simultaneously to build number sense.

Continuing the Activity

With less than ten minutes of math class left, the students were at many different stages in their work. Pam and I agreed they needed some time the following day to finish up their papers and share their work. For the moment, I decided to bring them back together to finish the game of Guess My Number before I left. I called for their attention.

"Now you have quite a bit of information about numbers whose digits add up to ten," I told them. "I've seen a lot of incredible work and thinking going on here. I'm going to give you an opportunity to put your knowledge to the test. You can use your papers to help you when we play Guess My Number. I have a secret number whose digits add up to ten. Who would like to take a guess?" Everyone signaled. I called on Andrea.

"Three hundred and twenty-five?"

"My number is less than 325," I responded.

"Two hundred and forty-four?" asked Joelle.

"My number is greater than 244," I told her.

"Two hundred and eighty?" Lisa guessed.

"You're right!" I said. "My number was 280. How many guesses did that take?"

"Three!" the class replied amidst high fives and grins.

"I guess your hard work and thinking really paid off," I said. "I'll try to think of another tricky rule next time."

CAREN ANSWERS YOUR QUESTIONS

Is this activity really that beneficial?

I feel I get a lot of mileage out of Guess My Number. I stop at various points during the game to ask questions that force the students to think about numbers and relative quantities. The mini-investigations I introduce (finding the numbers that end in zero or add up to ten) are a great assessment tool. By observing, listening, and questioning the students, I get a window into their number sense.

How can I use this activity in my classroom?

Guess My Number can be used as a warm-up throughout the year. You or your students just need to create new hints or different ranges of numbers. Fractions, decimals, and percents can even be incorporated. Spending time on related investigations is motivating and loaded with learning. Students are able to see relationships and con-nections between numbers and use

these patterns as a potent problem-solving tool.

What are some other hints I can use in games?

There are many options. It's sometimes useful to decide on the range first and then decide how many numbers you want to eliminate with your clue. For example, if the range is one through 100 and your clue is that your secret number is odd, half of the numbers in the range are still possibilities. If the range is one through 100 and your clue is that your secret number has two identical digits, you've narrowed the possibilities considerably.

You can also ask your students to brainstorm a list of clues they might use if they were leading the game. You'll be impressed at what they come up with and can use them in future games.

Why were you concerned that Carolina used the standard multiplication algorithm for 50×10?

First, both 50 and 10 are landmark numbers. Third and fourth graders need to be familiar with these numbers as quantities and as addends or multiples. Whether or not Carolina had much prior experience in dealing with two-digit multiplication, she should have had ways to think about 50 ten times or 10 fifty times.

Another part of number sense is efficiency. We don't want our students counting on their fingers into the thousands. It's just not efficient. Nor is it efficient to use a multistep paper-

and-pencil procedure for a problem that can be solved mentally in a matter of seconds.

The most disconcerting thing about Carolina's approach is her seeming to reach for a procedure before thinking about the numbers as quantities she can manipulate mentally. This is a symptom of the limitation of a traditional approach to teaching arithmetic skills. Children need the latitude to think freely about numbers and the encouragement to do so.

Estimation

We estimate every day. Do I have enough spaghetti to feed the six people who are coming for dinner? After I pay the rent and my bills, can I afford a weekend getaway? About how much punch should I buy for my daughter's birthday party? We answer these questions through a combination of mental computation and estimation. We don't usually pull out a calculator in order to figure the tip in a restaurant. We don't use paper and pencil to decide whether we have enough time to stop at the grocery store before meeting a friend for lunch. Estimating also helps us spot an answer that doesn't make sense. When the cashier rings up a dozen donuts and the total comes to over $20, we both know something is wrong.

It's extremely important that students have many opportunities to estimate, because the skill develops over time and with experience. The types of practice, discussion, and thinking associated with estimating help build number sense. Estimating helps students think of numbers as quantities, and opportunities to think about numbers in context are key. Context makes numbers real. It is also important for students to be able to decide when accuracy is essential and when an estimate will be good enough (or even better).

As students gain skill and experience with estimating in different contexts, they bring more and more number sense to tasks. They learn to use benchmarks—I know how many beans are in the small scoop so I can use that information to estimate how many beans are in the larger scoop. They begin to get a feel for quantities that are reasonable—there are 30 students in our class, and it looks like there are enough chairs in the auditorium for five classes. They develop a sense of relative magnitude—if I have 150 cookies, will eight serving plates be enough to hold them all?

The activities in this section focus on estimation. Through games, discussions, and investigations, students are asked to employ estimating skills. Students in the math classroom need occasions to delve into estimating tasks and analyze them in detail.

11

How Many Beans?

Overview

A jar, a scoop, and a quantity of beans are common materials that students can use in estimating activities. In this whole-class activity, students first estimate how many beans a jar will hold. Then, they determine the number of beans in a scoop and begin filling the jar with scoops of beans, adjusting their estimates with each scoop they add. Repeating this activity with different-sized jars, scoops, and beans can provide further experiences with estimation.

Materials Needed

A jar.
A scoop or a large spoon.
A bag of dried beans.

Teaching Directions

1. Show the students an empty jar, a scoop, and a bag of beans. Ask students to estimate how many beans the jar will hold and record their estimates.

2. Have the students determine how many beans a typical scoop holds.

3. Put a few scoops of beans in the jar and ask the students to calculate mentally approximately how many beans are in the jar and to explain their thinking.

4. Ask students to reestimate how many beans the jar will hold.

5. Repeat steps 3 and 4 until the jar is full.

6. Have students count the beans in the jar to find an exact total; ask them to compare this total with their final estimate.

IN THE CLASSROOM WITH RUSTY

Introducing the Activity

"About how many beans do you think will fit in this jar?" I asked Christina Stamford's fourth and fifth graders, holding up an empty jar in one hand and a bag of kidney beans in the other.

"You mean to the very top?" Tammy asked.

"Yes," I replied. "To the very top."

"*Exactly* how many beans or can we say *about* how many beans?" Joe asked.

"I'm interested in having you think about making a reasonable estimate, not in finding an exact answer," I said. "Finding the exact number of beans isn't important for this activity, or really for any reason. I can't think of a situation when knowing an exact number of beans is useful. But thinking about estimates is useful for your math learning."

I walked around the room, giving students a closer look at the jar and the beans. Students began to whisper their estimates to one another, then I called them back to attention. "Raise your hand if you want to share your estimate with us," I said. Lots of hands shot up. I began calling on students and recording their estimates on the chalkboard. Their estimates ranged from 100 to 1,000 beans, with most estimates between 100 and 350. Only one student, Mark, thought the jar would hold 1,000 beans.

When I'd written all their estimates on the board, I took a small

scoop, filled it with beans, and held up the scoop of beans and the jar so everyone could see. "I have a scoopful of beans and this empty jar," I said. "Can someone think of a way we could find out about how many beans will fit in the jar?"

"That's easy," Jaz said. "All you have to do is find out how many beans there are in the scoop, then fill the jar and count the scoops." Students nodded their agreement.

"You could just pour scoops in the jar and we could count by the number of beans in the scoop," added Jill.

"What if the cup held ten scoops of beans?" I asked. "How would that help us know about how many beans there are?" Again, hands shot up. This group seemed to find this an obvious question, but I wanted them to think and talk about what we needed to do in order to solve the problem.

"You have to use multiplication to figure that out," said Joe.

"What would you multiply?" I asked.

"You multiply the number of beans in each scoop times the number of scoops," he replied. Everyone seemed to be listening intently to Joe's explanation. (I often tell my students that it's important to be quiet while someone is explaining his or her thinking, but that it's more important to try to understand what's being said.)

"Does that make sense? Joe said that you need to multiply the number of beans by the number of scoops," I clarified. "So we need to know about how many beans there are in a scoop." I poured a scoopful of beans on the table where Megan was sitting and asked her to quickly count them. She reported there were 29 beans in the scoop. "Do you think every scoop will have the same number of beans in it?" I asked the class. They responded with a chorus of nos. "Why not?" I asked.

"Because some of the beans are probably big and some are little," Crystal explained. "They're different sizes."

"That's right, Crystal," I concurred. "Each scoop might have a slightly different number of beans."

I knew that taking one sample wasn't going to give us the best number for a typical scoopful. I could have given each pair of students in the class a scoopful of beans and had them count them, after which we could have taken an average to arrive at a typical number of beans per scoop. But to keep the focus of the activity on estimation and mental calculation, I decided to collect only one sample.

"I'm going to put scoopfuls of beans in the jar, and you're going to keep track of the number of beans," I continued. "But could we use another number of beans per scoop instead of 29, to make it easier for us to count?" I wanted the students to think about using friendly numbers in problem situations. Rounding the number of beans made sense, since they'd already realized that each scoop wouldn't have the same number of beans.

"How about 30 beans," suggested Barbara. "That's only one more, and 30 is easier to count by than 29."

"Watch carefully while I scoop beans into the jar," I instructed. "I want you to count the running total of beans out loud. Let's also keep track of

how many scoops fill the jar." I asked for a volunteer to record the numbers on the chalkboard. Then I took a level scoopful of beans and poured them into the jar. I held the jar up high, so everyone could see.

"Thirty!" the class chanted.

I poured three more scoopfuls of beans into the jar.

"Sixty, 90, 120," students counted. Skip counting by 30s was easy for these fourth and fifth graders. Everyone was engaged, their eyes fixed on the jar, which now held a layer of beans at the bottom.

"That's four scoops," I said. "Raise your hand if you'd like to change your estimate." About a fourth of the class raised their hand. "It's okay to change your estimate," I assured them. "In fact, I want you to think about your estimate every time you see me pour more scoops into the jar. Think about what your new estimate might be and why." Asking students to think about their new estimate based on what's already in the jar is important. Having a reference, or benchmark, to guide their thinking helps them produce reasonable estimates.

I poured three more scoops of beans into the jar as students counted: "One hundred and fifty, 180, 210." After seven scoops, the jar was over a third of the way filled. "About how many beans do you think the jar will hold now?" I asked, waiting until many hands were raised.

Wait time, as it's commonly referred to, is critical during class discussions. It allows students to formulate thoughtful ideas rather than quick guesses. It also helps you include the children who are not fast thinkers or strong personalities. Waiting isn't easy for me; my impulse is to call on the first student whose hand goes up. Although this moves the discussion along, it doesn't serve students' thinking. Children need time to think about numbers in order to develop their number sense.

"I think there will be about 500 beans," said Jill.

"Because . . . ," I prompted.

"Because there's already 210 beans and there's room for a lot more," she explained.

"Other ideas?" I asked.

"I think there's gonna be 500, too, because the jar isn't half full yet and 400 is twice 200, so it's gonna be more than 400," reported Nick.

I continued scooping beans into the jar. "Two hundred and forty, 270, 300," students chanted. I held up the jar and walked slowly through the room so that the students sitting in the back could get a closer look.

I returned to the front of the room and said, "We have ten scoops of beans in the jar. That's about 300 beans so far. Now how many beans do you think the jar will hold?"

"About two times 300," offered Simon.

"Why do you think that?" I asked.

"Because the jar's about half full and 300 times two is 600," he explained. Estimation often involves mental computation as a preliminary step. Lots of students nodded their head in agreement.

"I think about 600, too," said Jean. "But I thought about it different. We have ten scoops now, so we'll have about 20 scoops when we're done, and ten times 30 is 300, so 20 times 30 is 600."

Reba waved her hand vigorously after Jean's comment. "I don't think it'll be twice as much, because the jar is bigger at the top." She had noticed that the jar was slanted, so that its circumference continued to get bigger bottom to top. Reba's observation caused a stir, and a lot of hands were raised.

"I think the jar will hold more than 600 because of what Reba said," Josh agreed.

Josh's comment gave me an idea for a question that would prompt all the students to rethink their estimate. "Raise your hand if you think the jar will hold more than 600 beans," I said. Most students did. "Raise your hand if you think the jar will hold about 1,000 beans," I continued. This time no one raised a hand, not even Mark, who had originally thought the jar would hold 1,000 beans.

"I think it'll hold somewhere between 600 and 800," said Tammy. Estimating gives students a chance to compare quantities and think about number relationships. Children need to develop a feeling for what it means to use relative terms like *between, about, near, close*, and so on.

"Let's keep scooping so that we can find out about how many beans the jar will hold," I said. I put scoop after scoop into the jar as the students counted: "Three hundred and thirty, 360, 390, 420, 450, 480, 510, 540, 570." The entire class was focused on the jar, the scoop, and the beans. Comments were flying.

"It's almost full!" cried Jaime.

"It's going to be over 600!" Reba exclaimed.

"It's gonna hold another 30, probably 60!" Mark added.

I continued to scoop beans until the jar was full—22 scoopfuls, or about 660 beans.

A Class Discussion

After an initial moment of excitement, the room grew quiet. Then Reba raised her hand. "Are there really 660 beans in the jar?" she asked. Up until now, the activity had been about estimation, not exact answers. Reba was shifting the focus, and if she hadn't asked the question, I would have.

I handed the question back to her. "What do *you* think?"

"Well, I don't think so, because every scoop didn't really have exactly 30 beans," she said.

"Do you want to find out how many beans there really are in the jar?" I asked the class.

"Not really," Juan said. "They're only beans. Let's just stick with the estimate." Other students, however, were curious about how close our estimate was.

I used Juan's comment to propel the activity in another direction. In order to build number sense, children need to have opportunities to estimate and opportunities to be precise. They also need experience making decisions about how precise an answer needs to be, and this depends on the problem's context. "Maybe some of you aren't interested in finding the exact number of beans in the jar," I said, "but when *would* it be important to figure an exact answer? And when is an estimate good enough?" I allowed the students some time to think and talk about different situations that required estimates and exact answers, then I asked them to report their ideas. "So what do you think?"

"Well, I agree with Juan that with the beans we only have to have an estimate," said Simon. "But when I go to the store and buy something, I want to get the exact change when I pay for something."

"If the beans were like quarters or something, and we wanted to share them, I'd want to know exactly how many," said Megan.

"You need to be exact when you do your taxes, that's what my mom says," added Crystal.

"Sometimes my dad just estimates when he cooks," said Juan. "He just throws in a little of this and a little of that."

"So what about the beans?" I asked. "If an estimate is okay, how close is close enough? Our estimate is 660. How close do we have to be in order for our estimate to be reasonable?" This question stumped the class. I don't think they really understood what I was asking.

"If there are really 2,000 beans in the jar, would you be satisfied with our estimate of 660?" I asked.

"No!" they responded.

"Why not?" I asked.

"Because that's way off," said Jill. "It should be closer than that."

"What if the actual number of beans is 700? Would 660 be close enough then?" I asked. Students nodded, and seemed content with this amount of difference.

"I'd be happy with anything that was about 100 away," said Jill.

"Let's count them and see how many beans there are!" Nick piped up. So that we could accomplish Nick's suggestion quickly, I poured some beans on each table for partners to count. As pairs finished counting, I wrote the totals on the chalkboard. Together, we calculated that the jar held exactly 702 beans.

Continuing the Activity

I liked what had happened during the first experience with the jar, the beans, and the scoop: students had gotten experience with estimating and computing in context. Since skip counting by 30 had been easy for the students, when I returned to Christina's class the next day, I posed a similar problem that would challenge them in a different way. I brought with me the jar, the scoop, and the bag of red beans we'd used the day before. I also brought a bigger jar and a wider scoop.

I showed the class the new jar and scoop, and we compared them with the ones we'd used the day before. Students noticed that the new jar was taller and bigger around and that the new scoop had a wider mouth than the first one we'd used. I then asked them about how many beans the new jar would hold. I thought the students' estimates—ranging from 850 to 2,000—were better than their initial

estimates the previous day. Only one student, Tasha, had a significantly larger estimate—5,000 beans.

After I recorded their estimates on the chalkboard, I held up the new scoop. "This scoop holds about 40 beans," I told them. I wrote *about 40 beans per scoop* on the chalkboard. "I'm going to put some scoops into the jar, then I'm going to ask you a question about the beans." I carefully poured five scoops of beans into the jar.

"About how many beans are in the jar now?" I asked. This was the same question I'd asked the day before, only this time I didn't give them a chance to skip count. I waited very briefly, then called on Joanna.

"I did 40 times ten first, because I know that's 400, then I took half of that, which is 200," she explained.

"I just counted in my head by 40s," added José.

"Another idea?" I asked.

"I think there's about 200 beans in the jar now," said Branden. "I did four times five equals 20, then I added a zero and it's 200."

"Why did you add the zero?" I asked.

"Because it's not really four times five, but that makes it easier to do. I learned that you just look at it like it's four times five, and you add a zero, and you get the answer."

I had to stop and think. Did Branden really understand the numbers, or was he applying a trick or shortcut he'd learned? Although shortcuts can eliminate a lot of work, they can also prevent students from thinking about the numbers and what they really mean. I pressed on. "Can someone else explain why Branden's method makes sense?"

"It's not really four times five, it's 40 times five, and four times five is 20, and you add the zero from the 40 to the 20, and it's 200," explained Juli.

"What happens to a number when you add a zero to it?" I asked. "For example, when you add a zero to two, what happens to the two?"

"It becomes 20," said Courtney.

"How do two and 20 compare?" I asked.

"Twenty is a lot bigger," Megan responded.

"It's 18 more than two," added Ben.

"Twenty is ten times bigger than two, because two times ten is 20," Orlando explained.

"When you add a zero to the two it makes it ten times bigger, so if four times five is 20, then if you add a zero to 20 it's gonna be ten times bigger than 20, and that's 200," said Branden.

Sometimes I worry that a digression like this will lead us too far afield. In this instance, I think the conversation was worthwhile, because it helped both to clarify Branden's idea and to illustrate the importance of place value.

"Now that you know that there's about 200 beans in the jar so far, raise your hand if you want to change your original estimate," I said. Only about six students raised their hand.

I wrote *5 scoops = about 200 beans* on the chalkboard, then I put fifteen more scoopfuls into the jar. I held up the jar so everyone could see. It now held 20 scoops of beans, and it was a little over half full. I wanted to give the

students a new benchmark from which to make an estimate. I was also curious about how they would think about 20 times 40. "How many beans do you think are in the cup now?" I asked. When only a few hands popped up, I asked them to talk to the person next to them about the problem. Soon, there were lots of hands in the air. I called on Jill.

"There's about 800," she said. "Two times four is eight and 20 has one zero and 40 has one zero, so it's 800."

"Forty times ten is 400, so I doubled it to make 800," explained Orlando. "I remember us talking about 40 times ten before."

"I tried to count by 40s," added Najee. "But you were going too fast. So I did what Orlando did."

These students were in control of their own reasoning and calculations, and their explanations made me realize how important mental calculation is to number sense. After listening to several additional explanations, I wrote *20 scoops = about 800 beans* on the chalkboard. Then I walked through the room, showing the students the jar, which was now over half full of beans. As I made my way around, I posed a question. "How many beans do you think the jar will hold now?" I gave students time to mull this over, and there was lots of conversation. Then I called on Dave.

"Now I think the jar will hold 1,400 beans, because I think 600 more will fill the jar, and 800 plus 600 is 1,400," Dave said.

"I think the jar will hold about

1,200 beans, because it's over halfway full and there's about a quarter of the way to go," added Jill.

"I think the jar will hold 1,200 beans, because we're two thirds of the way with 800," explained Orlando.

"I think 1,300 beans, 'cause we're a little over halfway, so I think about 500 more will fill it, and 800 plus 500 is 1,300," said Chris.

"Other estimates?" I asked.

"I think the jar will hold 1,000, beans because there's one fourth of the way to go before we fill it," said Cheryl.

"What makes you think that?" I probed.

"Well, it's about three-fourths full now, so a couple hundred more would be 1,000," she replied. "There's about 250 something for each quarter of the jar."

"I think it looks about half full now, so my estimate is 1,600, 'cause 800 and 800 is 1,600," said Vanessa.

"I'm estimating 1,400, because there are 800 beans now and the jar is five-eighths full," said Nick.

"What made you think about eighths?" I asked. I was curious about whether Nick was just guessing or if he really had an understanding of fractions in this situation.

"Well, I used eighths because I wanted to be different than everyone else," he began. "The higher the denominator is, the more detail you can put into your estimate. I was just estimating when I thought five eighths."

"If the jar was half full, how many eighths would that be?" I probed.

"That would be four eighths," he

replied. "So it's a little more than half full now, so it's about five eighths."

"About how many beans would be in the jar if it were half full?" I continued.

"About 700," he said. "Seven hundred plus 700 is 1,400, and that's how many beans I think the jar will hold."

"About how many beans would be in the jar if it were two-eighths full?" I asked, pressing for more information about his understanding of eighths.

Nick thought for a couple of seconds, then replied, "About 350 beans." His thinking was solid. Sometimes probing questions can reveal a student's number sense. My conversation with Nick also gave other students an opportunity think about the problem in a different way.

A Writing Assignment

When the students had finished discussing their estimates, I told them I wanted them to explain their thinking in writing so that I could get some insight into their reasoning. I put two prompts on the chalkboard:

- Twenty scoops is about 800 beans because _____ .
- Now I think the cup will hold ____ beans because _____ .

The class wrote for the remainder of math period, about fifteen minutes. Before I left, I collected their papers and finished scooping beans into the cup. The cup held 31 scoopfuls, for a total of about 1,250 beans.

The papers were very revealing. Most of the students who had participated in our class discussions seemed to have pretty good number sense. Most estimated that there would be somewhere between 1,000 and 1,600 beans in the cup, and they supported their estimates with logical arguments that made sense. (Figures 11.1 and 11.2 are two examples.) Their reasonable estimates and calculation methods made me think

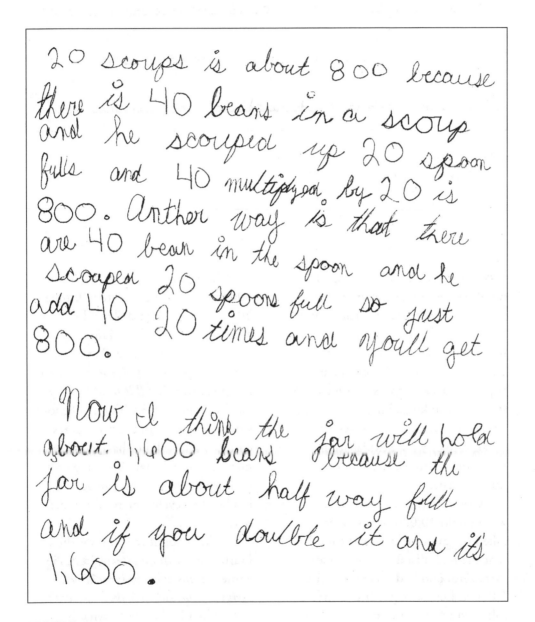

20 scoups is about 800 because there is 40 beans in a scoup and he scouped up 20 spoon fulls and 40 multipyed by 20 is 800. Anther way is that there are 40 bean in the spoon and he scouped 20 spoons full so just add 40 20 times and youll get 800.

Now I think the jar will hold about 1,600 beans because the jar is about half way full and if you double it and it's 1,600.

FIGURE 11.1

Megan explained why 20 scoops is about 800 beans.

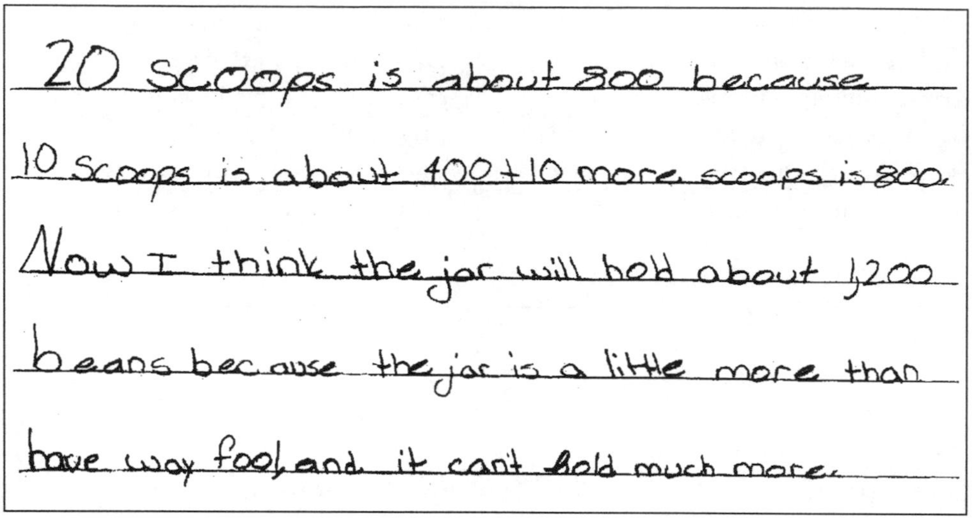

> 20 scoops is about 800 because
>
> 10 scoops is about 400 + 10 more scoops is 800.
>
> Now I think the jar will hold about 1,200
>
> beans because the jar is a little more than
>
> have way fool and it cant hold much more.

FIGURE 11.2

Orlando thought the jar would hold 1,200 beans because at two-thirds full the jar holds about 800 beans.

they had a good understanding of numbers and numerical operations.

A few enthusiastic participants in a class can sometimes give a false impression that everyone is at the same place. As I read the remaining papers, I saw soft spots in some of the students' thinking. There were three students whose estimates weren't reasonable or whose explanations raised questions for me about their number sense.

Crystal estimated that the cup would hold 10,000 beans. When I asked her about this later, I found that she had mistakenly added an extra zero, and had meant to write 1,000 as her estimate. If I hadn't followed up, I would have been left with a false assumption about her number sense.

Tasha's estimate was also 10,000.

Explaining why 20 scoops equaled 800 beans, Tasha calculated 20 times 40 using the standard algorithm. When I probed her thinking later, she stuck with this estimate: *Now I think the jar will hold 10,000 [beans] because it is 3 quarters in till it is all the way up.* (See figure 11.3.) It's possible for students to learn to use procedures correctly and still not have good number sense. In fact, focusing only on learning procedures can actually inhibit the development of number sense.

Mike thought the cup was three-fourths full with 800 beans in it. He wrote: *I think that the jar will hold about 700 because it looks littler than 800.* When I asked Mike what he meant, he looked puzzled. It was difficult for him to explain his thinking, and he seemed to lack

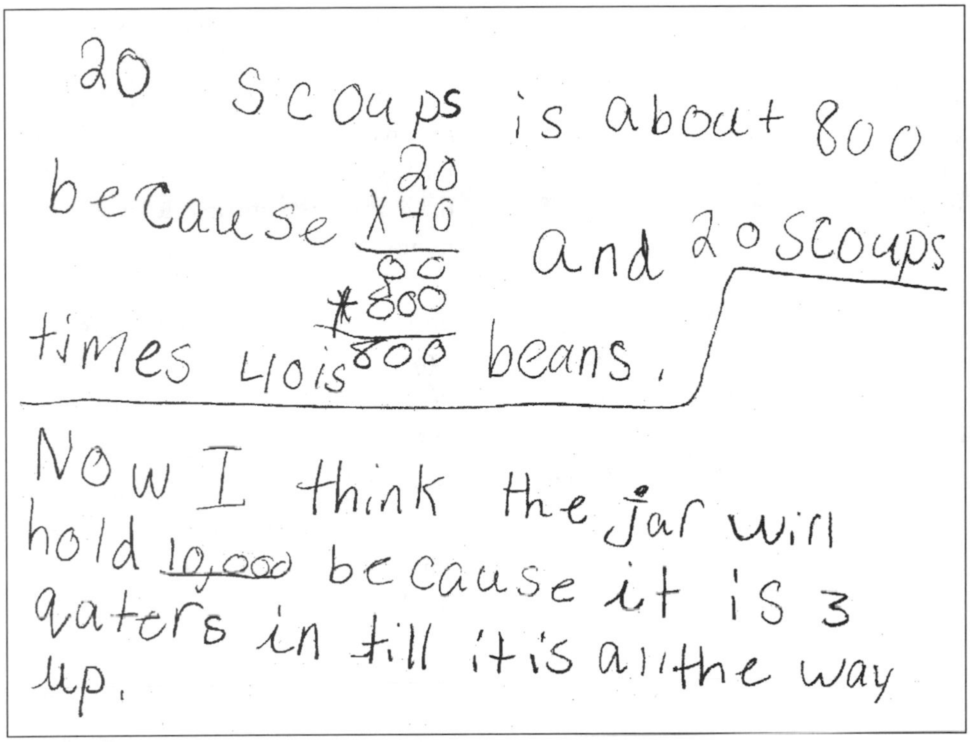

20 scoups is about 800
because
$$\begin{array}{r} 20 \\ \times 40 \\ \hline 80 \\ *800 \end{array}$$
and 20 scoups
times 40 is 800 beans.

Now I think the jar will
hold 10,000 because it is 3
qaters in till it is all the way
up.

FIGURE 11.3

Tasha's estimate for the number of beans is unreasonable.

confidence in his ability to reason with numbers.

There aren't always "quick fixes" for students like Tasha and Mike. Number sense develops over time, and children need regular opportunities to estimate, calculate mentally, reason with numbers, and hear others express their ideas. They need to experience activities like How Many Beans? so that they can see that numbers have meaning and are useful for solving problems. And students need to have the chance to build their confidence by working in environments where they feel safe taking risks and making mistakes.

RUSTY ANSWERS YOUR QUESTIONS

What is the purpose of this activity?

It has two important aspects. One is that it is an experience designed to improve estimation skills. During the activity, students are continually provided with benchmarks that help guide their thinking and improve their estimates. The first time I did the activity in Christina Stamford's classroom, for example, students were able to readjust their estimates several times, first after the jar held four scoops, then after it held seven scoops, again after ten scoops, and finally when it was full, at 20 scoops. Along the way, students readjusted their thinking based on the new mathematical information made available.

The other important aspect of the activity involves mental computation. To arrive at a reasonable estimate, students are required to calculate mentally as a preliminary step. For example, when the jar was about half full with ten scoops and about 300 beans, Simon offered this line of reasoning: "[There are] about two times 300, because the jar's about half full, and 300 times two is 600."

Is it important to use beans in this activity?

There's nothing magical about using beans; cubes or pennies work just as well. What's important is that these concrete objects provide a context for thinking about a problem. A math problem with a context is more meaningful for students and gives them a purpose for computing and estimating.

Whatever manipulatives you use help students view numbers as quantities and establish benchmarks from which to make estimates. For example, the first time I did the activity, when the jar was a little over a third of the way filled, it held about 210 beans. Students used this reference to guide their thinking when estimating how many beans the jar could hold. In other words, the beans helped them think mathematically

rather than make a wild guess. The manipulatives also give students a way to verify whether their final estimate is reasonable or not. Once they arrive at a final estimate, they are able to count the items and compare the total number to their estimate.

You mention that one sample isn't sufficient to find the best number of beans for a typical scoop. Can you say more about this?

As teachers, we make decisions based on the goals of the activity and the amount of time we have to teach it. In How Many Beans? one of my goals is for students to gain experience estimating and calculating mentally. The focus isn't on collecting and organizing data or learning about averaging. Finding the typical number of beans in a scoop is certainly important here, but finding the *best* number takes too much time.

How can I vary this activity?

There are many ways to structure an estimation activity. You could start with a jar full of beans (or cubes or whatever) and then ask your students to estimate the total number. After that, the students could count about half (or a fourth or an eighth) of the beans in the jar and then make another estimate of the total number.

No matter how the activity is structured, you can help your students develop their number sense by asking them to rethink their estimates along the way and to explain their reasoning once they've made an estimate.

You mentioned that there aren't always quick fixes for students like Tasha and Mike. What are some things you could have done to help them with this activity?

While all students should have access to the curriculum being taught, sometimes it's necessary to adjust an activity so that the numbers are smaller and more easily accessible. For example, I might have posed a similar, smaller problem for Tasha and Mike to solve. I think they would have benefited from thinking about fewer numbers of beans, say 100 or 200. This might have given them a better starting place from which to think about the numbers. Finding out what size number a student is comfortable or capable of working with is an important part of the assessment process.

Like all students, Tasha and Mike need many experiences over time in order to develop number sense. They also need opportunities to work with other students so that they have a chance to listen to different ways of thinking. In my classroom, I try to give struggling students some initial support before sending them off to work by themselves or with a partner. This support comes in different forms. Sometimes I'll ask a student questions that will stimulate his thinking. At other times I'll think out loud, modeling how I would approach a problem.

While we need to support struggling students, we also need to keep in mind that confusion is a natural and important part of the learning process. Just because a student is confused or having difficulty with one activity doesn't necessarily mean that a student is deficient or lacks number sense. Children must be allowed to make mistakes in a supportive environment and be given many opportunities to learn something new.

How can I assess students' number sense in this activity?

During the activity, I kept these questions in mind in order to assess students' number sense:

- Are their estimates reasonable or not?
- Are their estimates based on some mathematical reasoning?
- Are they improving their estimation skills through experience? Do they make use of benchmarks in order to improve on their estimates?
- How large or small a quantity of beans are they comfortable with?
- Are they able to calculate mentally? What strategies do they use? Do they use mental calculation to assist them in making better estimates?
- Do they use fractions when making estimates? Do they seem to understand the fractions they're using?

12 *Hit the Target*

Overview

While it is important for students to learn to multiply accurately, it is equally important for them to learn to estimate answers to multiplication problems. When students can estimate, they are better able to judge whether answers, in whatever way obtained, are reasonable. In this game, students work in pairs. They figure mentally or use a calculator to multiply numbers together to produce a product that falls within a predetermined range. The goal is to hit the target in as few steps as possible. (In a more advanced version of this activity, students often need to multiply using decimals—see extension 1, below.)

Materials Needed

A calculator for each pair of students.

Directions for Playing the Game

1. Players choose or are given a target range (800–850, for example), in keeping with the kinds of numbers they are comfortable with.

2. Player 1 chooses a number between 1 and 100 (50, for example).

3. Player 2 chooses another number to multiply the first number by, either mentally or with a calculator (50×10, for example), and player 1 verifies and records the result.

4. If the product doesn't hit the target range, player 2 goes back to the original number and multiplies it by another number (again, either mentally or with a calculator), and player 1 verifies and records the result.

5. Players repeat step 4 until the product falls within the target range.

6. Players repeat the game, this time alternating roles.

Sample Game Scenario

Target Range:	800–850
Starting Number:	50
$50 \times 10 = 500$	The number is too low.
$50 \times 20 = 1,000$	The number is too high.
$50 \times 15 = 750$	The number is closer but still too low.
$50 \times 17 = 850$	The number is within the target range.

Extensions

1. If the product doesn't fall within the target range, students use the product (not the original number) as their new starting number and determine what number to multiply it by to hit the target range. This version of the game often involves multiplying by decimals to get to the target. Before playing it, students should have spent some time exploring decimal numbers with calculators, seeing what happens when they multiply a number by another number that is less than one, what happens when they multiply a number by 1.5, etc.

2. Play Hit the Target using addition and subtraction rather than multiplication.

IN THE CLASSROOM WITH RUSTY

Introducing the Activity

"I have a new game I want to teach you called Hit the Target," I said, as I began the activity with Pam Long's sixth graders. "In this game, you'll use mental math and a calculator to multiply numbers.

"The game is called Hit the Target because the goal is to hit a target range—800 to 850, for example—by multiplying a starting number by some other numbers. The idea is to do this in as few multiplications as possible." I placed an overhead calculator on top of a blank transparency. I wrote *Hit the Target* at the top of the transparency, and then wrote *Target Range: 800–850.*

"Two people play," I continued. "Player 1 picks the starting number and player 2 mentally figures out what to multiply by to get into the target range. When you play, you and your partner take turns being player 1 and player 2. Would someone like to play Hit the Target with me?" Lots of hands wiggled in the air. "You be player 1, Mindy, and I'll be player 2," I said. "To play, we both have a few jobs." I pointed to the directions, which I'd written on the chalkboard beforehand:

1. Player 1 picks the starting number (1–100) and records it.
2. Player 2 chooses a number to multiply by.
3. Player 2 multiplies mentally.
4. Player 1 checks player 2's multiplication and records it.

5. If the product didn't hit the target, player 2 chooses another number to multiply by.

After reading the directions out loud, I said, "Mindy, give me a number between one and 100 to start with."

Mindy went up to the overhead projector. "How about two," she suggested, writing *2* on the projected transparency.

"Now I have to think of a number, any number, so that two times the number will give an answer that's between 800 and 850," I said to the class. "Raise your hand if you have a suggestion for me."

"Try multiplying by 425," said Gordon.

"Why did you suggest 425?" I asked.

"Because if you double 425, it's 850. It's easy," he answered. Mindy wrote $425 \times 2 = 850$ on the transparency.

"Gordon already checked the answer for me using mental math," she said. "You hit the target in one move!" Mindy returned to her seat.

"Thanks, Mindy," I said. "If Mindy and I were to continue with the game, we'd switch and I would be player 1 and she would be player 2. But this time, I'll be player 1 and the class will be player 2. I'm going to choose 12 to start." I wrote the number *12* on a new transparency. "Now you have to think of a number to multiply by 12 to hit the target," I reminded them. "Any suggestions?" The room was quiet. After several seconds, I asked a question to stimulate their thinking. "How about multiplying 12 by five?" I asked.

"That's only 60," said Anita. "You have to try a much bigger number."

"Well, how about 100 then?" I inquired. Students were shaking their heads in disagreement. "Why shouldn't you do that?" I probed.

"Because 12 times 100 is 1,200, and that's way over the target range," Katie said. "Let's try 12 times 50."

"Okay," I said to the class. "Multiply 12 times 50 mentally." I knew this would be challenging for some students, so I gave the class time to think about the problem. After more than half of the students had raised their hand, I called on Xavier.

"It's 600, because 12 times five is 60, and you have to do ten times more than that, and that would be 600," he reasoned.

Jenny did it another way. "Ten times 50 equals 500, and two more 50s make 600."

"I thought about it like this," Mindy said. "Twelve times ten is 120. Then you need five 120s. One hundred and twenty and 120 is 240; that's two. Two hundred and forty and 240 is 480; that's four. So 480 and another 120 is 600, because 480 plus 100 is 580 plus 20 more is 600."

I recorded *12 × 50 = 600* on the transparency, then verified the answer on the overhead calculator.

"Let's try a bigger number, like 70," Xavier suggested.

"What's the answer to 12 times 70?" I asked. I gave the students a moment and then called on Anne.

"If 12 times 50 is 600, then 12 times 60 is ten more 12s and that's

120, so 12 times 60 is 720," she explained. "So you go another 120, and you get 840, which is within the range."

Anne was building on what she already knew, 12 times 50, to think about 12 times 70. I recorded *70 × 12 = 840* on the transparency, then verified the answer on the calculator.

"Let's try it again," I said. "This time, I'll be player 2 and the class will be player 1." Nicky volunteered to come up to the front of the room to record for the class and use the overhead calculator to verify answers.

"Let's do 50," Michael suggested. Nicky recorded *50* on the transparency.

"I have to think of a number to multiply by 50 and get into the target range. I'd like you to help me think of a number," I said to the class. "Tell the person next to you what you think." I made a quick tour of the room, listening to students' ideas, then called them back together.

"I think you should multiply 14 times 50, because in the last game we figured that 12 times 50 is 600, and we need to go higher than that," said Michael.

"You're right, Michael," I said. "We need to multiply 50 by more than 12, since 12 times 50 is only 600." Michael nodded. "And your suggestion is to do 14 times 50," I added. "How much is 14 times 50? How could we figure that out mentally, class?"

"Oooh, that's hard," Gordon said.

I waited a moment and no hands were raised. I decided to model my thinking for the students, to help them get their mind around the problem.

"Listen to my idea and see if you can explain why it makes sense," I said. "I know that 12 times 50 is 600, that's twelve 50s. But I need two more 50s to get fourteen 50s, and two more 50s is 100 more. So 14 times 50 is 100 more than 600, and that's 700. Can someone explain my idea in your own words?"

"Well, to start with, we already figured out that 12 times 50 is 600," said Rebecca. "So 12 times 50 is like twelve 50s. It's like you're counting by 50s. So you keep counting up a couple more 50s, and that's 700."

"So we know that fourteen 50s won't get us into the target range," I said. Nicky recorded $14 \times 50 = 700$ on the transparency and checked the answer on the overhead calculator.

"Does anyone have an idea about where we could go from here?" I asked.

"Multiply 50 times 17, because 50 times 16 is 800, and you add another 50 to get 850," Jenny explained.

"How do you know that 50 times 16 is 800?" I asked.

"Well, in 100 there's two 50s, and split 16 in two you get eight, and eight times 100 is 800," she reasoned.

"You could do 50 times 16 or 17, because both answers are within the range," observed Rebecca.

"Do you think 50 times 18 would work?" I asked.

"That's too high," answered Don. "If 50 times 17 is 850, then 50 times 18 is 900, and that's above the range."

Again, Nicky recorded the equation, then checked the answer on the calculator.

"Let's do one more together, then you'll be able to play Hit the Target

with a partner," I told them. "Let's switch again. I'll be player 1, and the class will be player 2. I'm going to have you start with 75. Is there a friendly number you can multiply 75 by to give you a good start?"

Multiplying by "friendly" numbers is a strategy some students don't think of using. Suggesting strategies can be helpful, but I've learned that if students don't understand why a strategy works, they won't apply it to other situations in which it makes sense to do so. Since number sense is making "sense" of mathematics, it's important that students understand what they're doing.

"Seventy-five times ten is 750, and add another 75 and that's 825," said Anita. "Do 75 times 11, and you'll get within the range."

"Why did it make sense to multiply 75 by ten to start with?" I asked.

"Because the target range is 800 to 850, and multiplying 75 by ten makes it in the hundreds real fast. You add a zero to the 75 to make 750, because it's ten times bigger than that," she explained.

I wanted students to get the idea that there are many ways to calculate. "Is there another way to think about this?"

"Pretend 75 is like three quarters," said Anne. "So try to get up to 800 or 825 by counting by 75s in your head. Like 75 and 75 is 150, and four 75s is 300, and so on."

"You could divide 825 by the number and see what happens," added Michael.

"Tell us more," I prodded.

"Like, divide 825 by 75 and then you'll get the number you need to multiply with 75," he said. Michael knew that multiplication and division were related. Understanding relationships between numbers and between operations is an indicator of number sense.

I finished the game by recording the equation and checking the answer, then I explained to the class what they were to do next. "Now I'd like you to partner up and play Hit the Target," I said. "You and your partner need a calculator, a piece of paper, and a pencil." I then pointed to the directions for the game on the chalkboard and asked Gordon to read them aloud one more time. When he had finished, the students excitedly fished their calculators out of their desks and began.

Observing the Students

Anne and Nicky were partners, and Nicky had just given Anne the number 37 to start with. Anne was thinking out loud. "I know that 30 plus 30 plus 30 is 90," she mused. "So I know that 37 times three is a little over 100. I'll add 30s until I get there, because 30 is easier to count by. One, two, three, that's 100; four, five, six, that's 200, seven, eight, nine, that's 300. . . ." She continued this way until she got to twenty-one 30s, which makes 700. "So try 21 times 37 on the calculator," she said to Nicky.

"That's 777," reported Nicky.

"So I'll go a couple more. I'll try 23 times 37," Anne thought aloud.

Nicky pushed 23×37 into the calculator and got 851 for an answer. "Man!" Anne moaned. "Just one over! I'll try 37 times 22." Nicky tested Anne's idea, and both girls shouted, "Yes! That's it!"

Nicole and Anita were struggling with the number 72. "Anita gave me the number 72 to start with, and I multiplied 72 times 12 and got 864," Nicole reported. "Then I multiplied 72 times 11, and that's 792! So anywhere I go I'm over or under the target range." Anita and Nicole were on the verge of bumping into decimals.

While I wanted to avoid explaining or giving away too much, I also wanted to prod them just enough so that they could think for themselves. This balancing act between how much to explain and how much time and space to give students to explore on their own is always a challenge. "So what can you do?" I asked.

"Nothing, I'm stuck," she replied.

"You need something between 11 and 12," I hinted.

"I don't get it," said Anita. "There's nothing we can use between 11 and 12 to multiply."

"If you had a ruler, what would be between 11 and 12?" I asked.

"Oh!" Nicole exclaimed, "11 and a half!"

"What's 11 and a half on the calculator?" I asked.

"That's 11 point five," said Anita. Nicole quickly multiplied 11.5 times 72 and got 828.

Michael and Don encountered a similar problem with the number 99. "I'm working with the number Don gave me, which is 99," said Michael. "Ninety-nine times nine is 891, and 99 times eight is 792. I can't get in the range."

"What's between eight and nine?" I asked.

"Eight point five?" Michael said, smiling. He multiplied 99 times 8.5 and got 841.5.

When I visited Cam, he was trying to think of a number to multiply by the starting number, nine. Cam struggles with arithmetic and often needs help getting started. His partner, Mitch, didn't seem to know how to help.

"Is there a number that's close to nine and friendlier to start with?" I asked.

He thought for a moment, then hesitantly said, "Ten?"

"Yes, let's start with ten," I confirmed. "We want to get an answer between 800 and 850. Let's focus on getting to 800. What can we multiply by ten to get to 800?" Cam stared into space, wearing that look that's so familiar when students haven't made sense of an idea. I posed a question that I hoped would stretch his thinking or at least give him a way into the problem. "What's ten times ten?" I asked.

"One hundred," he replied.

"How about ten times 20?" I continued.

"Two hundred?" he said.

I pressed on. "Ten times 30?"

"Oh, I get it!" he exclaimed, beaming. He continued until he got to ten times 80.

"Now we're at 800," I said, "but we need to multiply by nine, not ten."

With a little help, Cam multiplied nine times 80 by subtracting 80 from 800 to get 720 and realized he needed to go higher. With Mitch's help, Cam used trial and error to make his way to 89 times nine and was able to get into the target range.

At another table, Katie wanted to start with 99.5 just for the challenge!

A Class Discussion

After about twenty-five minutes, I called the class together for a discussion. "Did anything surprise you while you were playing Hit the Target?" I asked.

"All the numbers we used were easy," Gordon reported.

"What numbers did you use?" I asked.

Gordon scanned his paper. "Twenty, 60, 90, and eight," he said.

"I think even numbers are easier to start with," said Jenny. "Numbers like 37 or 77 are kind of hard. Whenever my partner gave me a number like that, I rounded it off to an easier number and worked from there."

"I think higher numbers are easier to work with," said Terry. "Like if you start with 85, you can multiply that by big numbers and it's easier to think about getting to the target range."

"When we started with 72, we had to multiply it by 11 point five on the calculator to hit the target," said Mindy. "We forgot that there were numbers between 11 and 12, then we remembered about decimals."

"Raise your hand if you had to use

decimals in this game," I said. Several hands went up. "What if we changed the rules of the game so that your partner could give you any starting number, not just numbers between one and 100?" I wondered. "How would that change the game?"

"Let's try it!" Blanca said. "How about starting with a number bigger than the target range." Blanca's idea fit perfectly with where I was going. If she hadn't made the suggestion, I would have done so.

"Okay, let's start with 1,200," I said. "You and your partner use your calculators and explore this problem. Start with 1,200 and see if there's a number you can multiply it by to hit the target."

This exploration was initially confusing and challenging. I let the students struggle as they experimented with lots of different numbers. After several minutes, I called for their attention. "What did you find out?" I asked.

"I realized that you can't multiply 1,200 by a whole number or you'd get a larger number than 1,200," said Jenny.

"You have to multiply by a decimal number, and it's hard," added Xavier. "We tried all sorts of things."

"Was anyone able to hit the target?" I asked.

"We knew that point five is a half, so we multiplied point five by 1,200 and got 600," said Katie.

"Let's try it," I suggested. Students tested Katie's idea on their calculator.

"It's like dividing by two," observed Michael.

"What did you do then?" I asked Katie.

"Then we multiplied 1,200 by point six and got 720," she replied. "We kept going, multiplying next by point seven, and we hit the target!"

"I noticed that when you multiply a number by a decimal, you get a smaller number," said Brennon.

"Is that always true?" I asked. Brennon looked puzzled, as did several other students. "Eight point five is a decimal number that's greater than one," I said. "Try multiplying eight point five by five and see what happens."

"I got 42 point five!" several students chorused.

"What's another decimal number that's greater than one?" I asked.

"How about five point three?" suggested Anne.

"Multiply five point three by ten and see if the answer is larger or smaller than ten," I said. "Make a prediction first." After several seconds, lots of hands were raised. I called on Jenny.

"The answer's larger than ten," she said.

"When you multiply a number by a decimal number that's smaller than one, the answer will be smaller," Katie concluded. "That's what we did when we multiplied 1,200 times point five."

This spontaneous exploration in the activity was exciting for the students. It was a detour that I hadn't expected to make, but it was worthwhile because it gave students an insight into decimal numbers. In order to allow my students to take the activity in different directions, I have to be familiar with the mathematics involved and flexible in my approach to teaching.

A Writing Assignment

I then asked the students to write about the game. On the chalkboard, I listed several questions they could use to help them get started:

- What did you like about Hit the Target?
- What was easy?
- What was difficult?
- What surprised you?
- What methods did you use to multiply numbers mentally?
- If you used decimals, what did you learn?

Cam wrote: *When I played hit the target with David the hardest one that he gave me was 17. That took me more than 3 tries to figure it out. First I guessed 17 × 90 which equals 1190. Finally I guessed 17 × 40 which is 680 so then I knew it had to be in the 50s so I chose 17 × 50 which is 850.*

Rebecca wrote: *I like Hit the Target. It isn't easy sometimes, but I like how it gets your mind thinking.*

Michael wrote: *This was a pretty fun game. I like mostly because I'm good at the game. I got all the ones he gave me on the first try. Except when he gave me 95.5. That was the only hard one. Some of my strategys were if he gave me a number between 80–85, I would multiply in my head. If he gave me a number under that but in the 70s, I would multiply that by 10.5.*

Additional examples of student work are shown in figures 12.1 through 12.4.

> Hit The Target
>
> I liked this game because it was challenging Melissa gave me. 81. I knew 80 x 10 was 800 so I used 10.5. I got 850.5. I knew I had to go down so I did 81 x 10.3 and I got 834.3 I could have done 81 x 10 and got 810 but I wanted to see if you could use decimals to find out the answer. Then Melissa gave me 67. 67 is kind of in the middle so I I decided to use 14. I got 938 so I decided to use 11. It was 737. That was too low so I used 12 and got 804.

FIGURE 12.1

Katie used decimal numbers while playing Hit the Target.

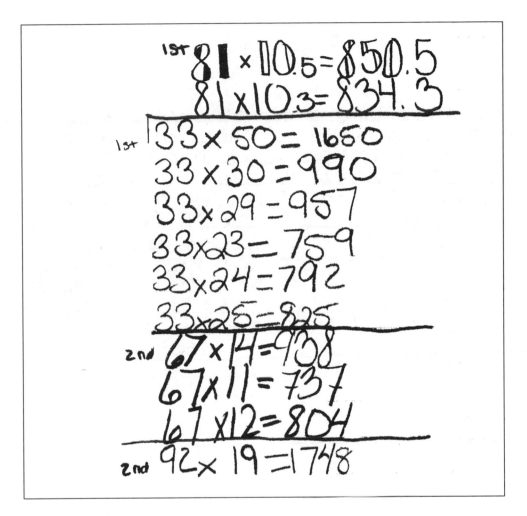

¹ˢᵗ 81 × 10.5 = 850.5
81 × 10.3 = 834.3

1ˢᵗ 33 × 50 = 1650
33 × 30 = 990
33 × 29 = 957
33 × 23 = 759
33 × 24 = 792
33 × 25 = 825

2ⁿᵈ 67 × 14 = 938
67 × 11 = 737
67 × 12 = 804

2ⁿᵈ 92 × 19 = 1748

FIGURE 12.2

Katie and Mindy's score sheet for Hit the Target.

Hit the target

This game helps me with my mental Math. And it helped me mult. with decimals. Like on my Game #2 my partner Nicole said 7½. So I mult. 72 and 12 and it equaled up to 864. Then I tried 72×11 = and it equaled 792. Nicole and I were confused so we call Ms Tracy and she gave us a hint. To use decimals Then I did 72×11.5 = 828. It helped me a lot. I think this game is a great game to use your math skills.

FIGURE 12.3

Anita noticed that Hit the Target helped with her mental math skills.

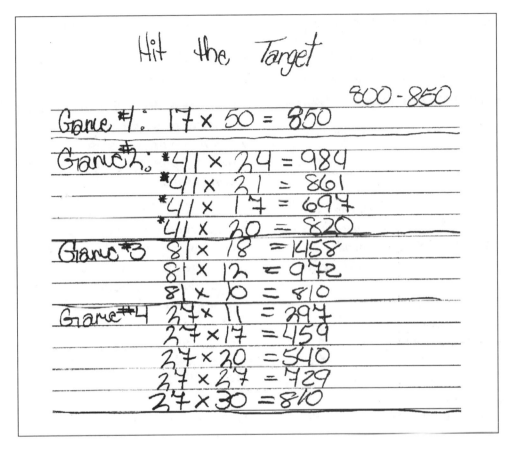

Hit the Target

800 - 850

Game #1: 17 × 50 = 850

Game #2: *41 × 24 = 984
         *41 × 21 = 861
         *41 × 17 = 697
         *41 × 20 = 820

Game #3 81 × 18 = 1458
         81 × 12 = 972
         81 × 10 = 810

Game #4 27 × 11 = 297
         27 × 17 = 459
         27 × 20 = 540
         27 × 27 = 729
         27 × 30 = 810

FIGURE 12.4
Nicole's score sheet for Hit the Target.

RUSTY ANSWERS YOUR QUESTIONS

How does this game help develop students' number sense?

When students rely on their intuitive reasoning about numbers and operations, they're using their number sense. The focus on estimation and mental calculation in this activity helps students develop this intuition.

After sixth graders had learned the game, Pam Long played Hit the Target with them for several weeks at the beginning of math class. She changed the target range frequently and reported that the experimentation with numbers called for in the game helped improve students' estimation and mental computation skills. Most important, she said, the game required students to calculate for a purpose and to apply multiplication meaningfully and flexibly.

When students estimate while playing Hit the Target, they have opportunities to compare numbers and think about number relationships. Forming an estimate also involves the student in mental computation as a preliminary step. For example, if the target range is 800–850 and the starting number is 50, a game might play out like this:

$50 \times 10 = 500$ *The number is too low.*

$50 \times 20 = 1,000$ *The number is too high.*

$50 \times 15 = 750$ *The number is closer but still too low.*

$50 \times 17 = 850$ *The number is within the target range.*

With each calculation, the player is thinking about the product and comparing it to the target range. By estimating, she produces an approximate answer, one that is "close enough" to allow her to decide *What do I do next in order to get into the target range?*

Calculating mentally helps students develop their own strategies for applying operations and helps them think flexibly. When I used the activity in Pam Long's classroom, for example, we were trying to hit the target range of 800–850 by using 75 as a starting number. Anita said, "Seventy-five times ten is 750 and add another 75 and that's 825." Anne thought about money when solving the problem: "Pretend 75 is like three quarters. So try to get up to 800 or 825 by counting by 75s in your head. Like 75 and 75 is 150, and four 75s is 300, and so on." Michael took a completely different approach. He suggested that we divide 825 by 75 to get the number you need to multiply 75 by. All three

students were solving the problem in a way that made sense to them. Calculating mentally facilitates these unique ways of making sense.

What are some questions I could ask that would stimulate students' thinking about the mathematics in this game?

As a teacher, you play an important role in building students' number sense. One way to help facilitate the development of number sense is to ask questions that require more than a right answer and that can prompt students to explore a mathematical idea. The following questions, which can be asked while students are playing Hit the Target, during a class discussion after the game, or as prompts for a writing assignment, will help you stimulate students' thinking and generate important discussions:

- What numbers were difficult to start with and which were easy? Why?
- What strategies did you use when calculating mentally? Explain your strategy.
- Did you change the target range? If so, what new target range did you use? How did the target ranges compare?
- Did you ever start with a number that was greater than the target range? If you did, explain what happened.
- How did the calculator help you in playing this game?
- Did you have to use decimal numbers in the game? If you did, explain what happened.

13

In the Ballpark

Overview

While many estimation activities involve students with thinking about whole numbers, this activity engages them in thinking about fractions and percents. Students first think about real-world examples for various quantities—less than $1/4$, about $2/3$, close to 33%, and so on. They then analyze other real-world examples and apply them to the students in their class.

Materials Needed

9 pieces of chart paper, each bearing a label:

> less than $1/4$
> about $1/3$
> about $1/2$
> about $2/3$
> about $3/4$
> about 25%
> close to 33%
> a little less than 50%
> more than 75%

$8 1/2$-by-11-inch sheets of paper labeled with different categories (*are only children, have an older brother, had cereal for breakfast,* etc.)

Teaching Directions

1. Post the sheets of labeled chart paper, in nonconsecutive order, along the front of the room.

2. Have students generate real-life examples of things that would fit under each quantitative heading.

3. Present the students with one of your predetermined categories, have them apply it to the students in the class, and ask them to discuss which quantitative heading it fits under and why.

4. Show the students the rest of your predetermined categories and have them choose one to explore and write about.

IN THE CLASSROOM WITH CAREN

Introducing the Activity

I posted nine pieces of chart paper at the front of Pam Long's sixth-grade classroom, in this order: *about $^1/_2$, less than $^1/_4$, about $^1/_3$, about $^3/_4$, a little less than 50%, about 25%, close to 33%, about $^2/_3$, more than 75%.* "Okay," I said to the class, "the posters taped on the chalkboard represent ballparks. Does anyone know what I mean by ballpark here?"

"It means about," Rafael responded.

"Like estimating a number," Nida added.

"Right," I replied. "When I say *Give me the ballpark price of that car* or *What's the ballpark number of kids in this school?* I want to know about how much or about how many. The papers I put up on your chalkboard are some ballpark numbers for you to think about. Can anyone think of a real-life example of something that fits under one of these categories?" Sensing some hesitation and seeing quite a few puzzled looks, I narrowed the question. Pointing to the sheet that said *about $^1/_2$,* I said, "Think about this school. Is there something here at school that you can say is about one half?"

Mick brightened. "There's about one-half girls and one-half boys at school."

"Not in our class," countered Tanetta. "We have way more girls in our class."

"But what about the whole school?" I asked. "There are probably some classes that have more girls and others that have more boys. Do you think overall in the whole school it's safe to say about half of the students are girls and half are boys?"

"I guess *about* a half," Tanetta conceded.

"What are some other real-life examples that might fit under one of these ballparks?" I continued.

"I know," offered Guillermo. "More than 75 percent of the kids play soccer at recess." While I personally had not spent a lot of time with the kids at recess, the nods of assent from the rest of the class indicated that soccer was indeed a popular activity.

Sariah piggybacked on Guillermo's recess estimate. "Less than one fourth play double Dutch at recess," she volunteered.

"And less than one fourth eat lunch at the picnic tables," Leu added. "Almost everyone likes to eat in the cafeteria."

Now that the students understood my original question, I widened the field. "Okay, so now think about examples outside school," I told the class. "Take a few minutes to talk to your neighbors and see whether you can come up with an example or two for each of the ballparks." I let the students talk with one another at their tables and then called them back to attention. "Who has an example?" I asked.

Kathy raised her hand. "We think about half of the people in the United States like pizza," she reported.

Quoch's table had talked about

pets. "About one third of the families in Oceanside have dogs," he predicted.

Brenda had a pie comparison. "When you cut up a pie for people to eat, each piece is less than one fourth of the pie."

I made sure the students provided at least one example for each ballpark posted, writing their ideas on the appropriate sheet. Then I continued to explain the activity. "Here's what's going to happen now. I have some pieces of paper with me on which I've written some categories of things. When I hold up the first category, your job is to think about which of these ballpark numbers the category belongs under." I held up the first piece of paper, which said *Boys in the room.* "Now take a few minutes to talk at your tables about where you think *Boys in the room* fits. And when you talk to each other, make sure you're explaining your thinking, not just telling answers. It's the thinking that's really important here and your reasons for your answers."

I circulated among the tables as the students discussed where *Boys in the room* might fit. All students began talking eagerly and animatedly, but the effectiveness of their discussions varied greatly. Some students fixated on determining the exact number of boys in the class. They counted and recounted the boys present and identified who was missing. Other students quickly agreed that there were fewer boys than girls in the class, eliminated the *about* $\frac{1}{2}$ option, and concentrated on identifying which of the other categories could be used to quantify the number of boys. I called

the class back together and asked students to share their ideas.

Alicia began. "I think it's about one third," she announced, "because there aren't as many boys as girls in the class."

"It could be less than one fourth," countered Alberto.

"Why do you think that?" I asked him.

"There are nine boys in the class and 17 or 18 girls," he explained. Although the numbers didn't support his idea, I decided not to push him at this point but to check in with him later. My goal was to explore different ways to think about the question. I looked around the room and counted the boys. "I just counted nine boys in the room. How many people are there in the room altogether?" After a moment of counting, we determined that there were 26 people in the room, including the students and the teachers.

A Writing Assignment

"Okay," I said, "so there are nine boys out of 26 people altogether." I wrote $\frac{9}{26}$ on a projected transparency. "I'm going to give you a few minutes for a quickwrite. Each of you will write your ideas about which ballpark you think $\frac{9}{26}$ is closest to. Don't just write an answer. Explain why you chose the ballpark you did."

"Can we make a picture to show it?" Mary asked.

"Sure, a picture or diagram is a great way to show an idea," I replied, "but you'll also need to write some words to explain your picture and how it helps you."

I gave the class about ten minutes for their quickwrite. There were two reasonable options: *close to 33%* and *about ⅓*. I wondered whether anyone would mention both, but no one did. But the papers were interesting. Gary used words and a picture to explain why he chose *close to 33%* (see figure 13.1). Alicia drew a pie graph divided into 26 sections and shaded nine of them, showing that it was close to ⅓ (see figure 13.2). She also rounded 26 to 27 in her written explanation. Even the papers of the students who did not choose the most reasonable ballpark provided useful information about their number sense.

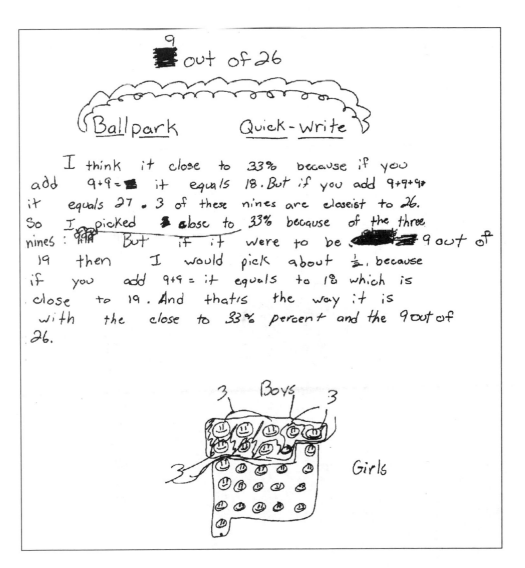

FIGURE 13.1
Gary told why ⁹/₂₆ is close to 33%.

Ballpark Quick-Write

1. 19 out of 26

I think about ⅓ because if
9 × 3 = 27 and 27 − 26 = 1. So
it is about ⅓ because
1 of those thirds is 9,
than 3 of those
thirds is 27. So
it is about ⅓.
Plus, there is not
that much boys
in the class.

about ½

a little less
then 50%

less then
¼

about ⅓

more then
75%

close
to 33%

SO
9 out of 26
is about

$$\frac{1}{3}.$$

FIGURE 13.2

*Alicia used a pie graph to help with her
estimate.*

A Class Discussion

"Okay," I told the class, "now you're going to do some work at your tables. You're going to have some choices about which problem to work on. I have three topics for you."

I held up three more of the category papers:

> *Are wearing tennis shoes*
> *Had cereal for breakfast*
> *Have a younger sister*

I like to provide students with choices when possible. Offering several options rather than dictating one gives students more independence and ownership. In this instance the subject of the hypothesis didn't matter: I would be able to see the students' ideas about numbers regardless of the topic they chose.

I explained the task. "You are going to choose one of these categories and decide which ballpark it fits in. Remember, we are talking about the people in the room right now. So you need to think about what fraction or percent of people in the room are wearing tennis shoes or had cereal this morning or have a younger sister. Spend a little time talking at your tables about each of these. Then you're going to pick one to concentrate on. Your job will be to write about the one you chose and explain where you think it fits. Are there any questions?"

Mick raised his hand. "Ms. Holtzman, when you say tennis shoes, do you mean sneakers or high tops or platforms or what?"

I was glad I had taken the time to review the activity before I sent the students off to work on their own. It's important to clarify language and expectations at the outset. "Well, I guess I haven't really thought deeply enough about what it means to be a tennis shoe," I confessed. I took the paper containing the too general category, crossed out the word *tennis,* and wrote *PE* in its place. "Here's the new way to think about it," I explained. "Focus on whether or not the shoes would be appropriate for you to wear during PE. There are some shoes that are okay for PE and others that are not. What fraction or percent of people in the room right now are wearing shoes that are PE approved? Does that make it clearer?"

The ensuing nods and murmurs indicated that they understood but were disappointed that a potentially exciting discussion about footwear had been squelched. "So, talk at your tables about these three categories. Then decide which one you're going to focus on. Try to figure out which ballpark it fits in. Be prepared to explain how you decided on your answer." The students began talking and working at their tables. I went from table to table, checking in and helping students refocus.

Another Writing Assignment

About fifteen minutes before the lunch break, I made an announcement. "You've had some time to talk about these three categories at your table and choose one to think about more. Now it's time for everyone to concentrate on writing your ideas. Let's take some quiet time so that everyone has a chance to get some ideas down on paper."

I collected the papers before the students went to lunch. Interestingly, all three choices received about equal attention. The papers showed a variety of approaches and a range of thinking.

Some of the students used empirical information exclusively to explain their ballpark choice. Mary wrote, *About 75% of the people in this class are wearing P.E. shoes because I took a peek under everybody's desk.* Calvin used his own experiences as well. He wrote, *I think about ¹/₂ the class has a younger sister because I know 9 people and 5 of them have a younger sister. Since there's more than 9 people in the class I think it's about ¹/₂.*

Several of the students used a broader generalization as a rationale for their decision. Although the task focused on people in the classroom, these students started with a bigger picture and then worked back to the smaller. (For some reason, this type of broad thinking occurred mostly in connection with the breakfast cereal category.) Emma was thinking nutritionally. She explained, *About ¹/₃ of the kids in my class eat cereal for breakfast. That is because when kids get older they need more to eat, not just cereal.* Nida had a global perspective (see figure 13.3): *I choosed cereal. My*

ballpark is close to 33% because every week day kids around the world are getting up early for school. We don't get enough time to eat cereal so we want something on the go so we eat something we like—toast—and we can eat it quickly. She included illustrations to emphasize the morning-rush breakfast dilemma.

Many students worked on the PE shoe category. Sariah included a written explanation and a picture on her paper (see figure 13.4). She imagined what the two groups (wearing PE shoes and not wearing PE shoes) would look like if they were on two different soccer teams. She wrote, *I think that more than 75% of the class is wearing P.E. shoes today, because if you were playing a soccer game, and you needed to have even teams. So if you took the people that were wearing P.E. shoes for a team and boots, high heels, ect. in another team to make two teams it would be very uneven.*

The papers gave me an insight into the students' number sense, particularly their estimation strategies. Did they use sample data to predict? Which ballpark did they equate with which numbers? Did they compare whole numbers with fractions and decimals? How? The assessment possibilities of this activity are rich, and repeated discussions and writing assignments will definitely strengthen the students' estimating capabilities.

FIGURE 13.3
Nida explained the breakfast dilemma.

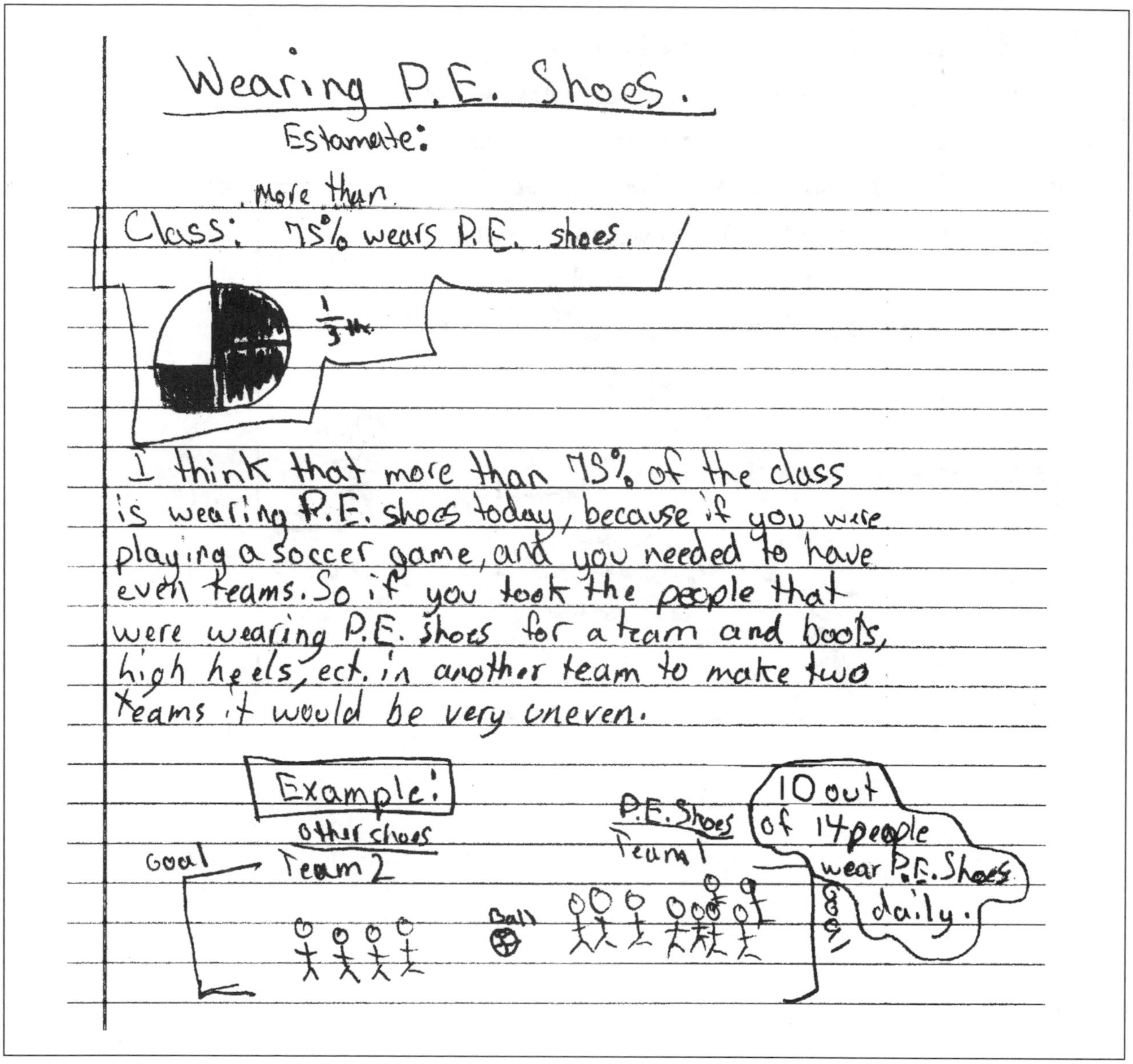

Wearing P.E. Shoes.

Estamate:

More than

Class: 75% wears P.E. shoes.

$\frac{1}{3}$ the

I think that more than 75% of the class is wearing P.E. shoes today, because if you were playing a soccer game, and you needed to have even teams. So if you took the people that were wearing P.E. shoes for a team and boots, high heels, ect. in another team to make two teams it would be very uneven.

Example:

Other shoes
Team 2

Goal

P.E. Shoes
Team 1

10 out of 14 people wear P.E. Shoes daily.

Ball

FIGURE 13.4

Sariah pictured uneven soccer teams.

CAREN ANSWERS YOUR QUESTIONS

How does this activity promote the development of number sense?

Estimation requires a feel for quantities, relative magnitude, and benchmarks. It's vital for students to have many opportunities to estimate in math class, so that they will develop these abilities. This activity gives students a chance to estimate and also to discuss and write about their thinking: not only are they practicing estimation, they are being given opportunities to think about estimation in different ways. Thinking about their own methods of estimating and listening to their classmates' ideas build their estimation proficiency.

Many estimation activities involve guessing how many of something. This activity asks students to think about estimation in a different way. Presenting the students with real situations and a number of ballparks requires them to think about relative quantities. They need to collect data or use a benchmark to help them make sense of the situation and choose the most reasonable quantification. In most instances students do some mental computation to help them choose the most reasonable estimate.

Why did you choose these particular "ballparks"?

I deliberately chose "landmark" fractions and percents. Just as there are landmark whole numbers (10, 25, 50, 75, 100),

there are important fraction and percent benchmarks. Once students have a solid grasp of these numbers, they are better able to negotiate the number system. They can handle unfamiliar numbers by comparing them with more familiar benchmarks.

These students seemed more comfortable with the fraction ballparks than with the percents. This is not surprising at the beginning of sixth grade. I was curious whether anyone would notice that several of the fraction ballparks were essentially the same as the percentage ones. No one mentioned it. An interesting follow-up activity would be to ask the students to put the ballpark choices in ascending order or to find ones that were very close to each other.

Can this activity be adapted for other grade levels?

With these sixth graders, I used ballparks that involved fractions and percents. However, you can choose any numbers. In a third-grade class, you might use *close to 10, close to 20, close to 50,* and *close to 100.* Ballparks can even be ranges of numbers: *1–50, 51–100,* etc. As students develop solid foundations and clear pictures of what numbers look like, use more challenging quantifications.

Students can also generate their own ballparks or their own topics. You can devote part of a class session to brainstorming ideas of things to explore and categorize. Or you can present a subject such as *number of crayons in the room* and ask students to name a ballpark that seems reasonable to them.